CLASSIC *f*M

CLASSIC
Romance

Writing from the Heart

CLASSIC *f*M

CLASSIC
Romance
Writing from the Heart

COMPILED
BY

Nick Bailey

Hodder & Stoughton

Script editor: Peter Mackie

First published in 1998 by Hodder and Stoughton
A division of Hodder Headline PLC

10 9 8 7 6 5 4 3 2 1

A CIP catalogue record for this title is
available from the British Library

ISBN 0 340 73849 9

Typeset by Palimpsest Book Production Limited,
Polmont, Stirlingshire
Printed and bound in Great Britain by
Clays Ltd, St Ives plc

Hodder and Stoughton
A division of Hodder Headline PLC
338 Euston Road
London NW1 3BH

To Kate and Robert

CONTENTS

True Romance

✻   ✻   ✻

CONTENTS

What Might Have Been

Love Everlasting

CLASSIC ROMANCE

INTRODUCTION

S HAKESPEARE got it about right when he wrote those opening lines to *Twelfth Night*, 'If music be the food of love, play on.' Since *Classic Romance* started on Classic FM in September 1992 we have heard how there have been many occasions when music has been an integral part of a relationship. It could be the opening gambit in a conversation or a shared moment at a concert. It's often been used as a time for reflection when major decisions are made – a proposal, leaving an unhappy liaison, or going abroad to start a new life. And then of course there's the wedding music. Even the most unromantic and unmusical of couples will choose their wedding music with great care. Music, and in particular classical music, is very good at capturing a mood and creating the right atmosphere for that special occasion. So it made good sense for our original programme controller, Michael Bukht, to invent a programme that combined classical music with romantic memories. A simple formula that has been incredibly successful, making *Classic Romance* Classic FM's most popular programme, with almost a million listeners every week. It's also picked up two major awards – a Sony silver in 1995, and in 1996 it was voted the radio programme of the year by the Television and Radio Industries Club.

It is now into its seventh year, and the letters and e-mails show no signs of abating. Obviously we can't use them all, but I or my producer Amanda Lewis have read every one. And that's a lot of reading. I've worked out that we've received well over fifteen thousand letters since the show started!

Choosing the letters for a weekly three-hour programme is hard enough, so you can imagine how hard it was to choose a good balance of correspondence for this book. Quite a few writers over the years have said they thought it unlikely that their letter would be used for the programme, but they were just glad we had time to read it ourselves. Many of the letters are almost confessional and make quite poignant reading. We seem to have had every type of romance imaginable, including love at first sight, love the second time around, love rekindled, what might have been, and unrequited love. *Classic Romance* on occasion has even managed to bring people together, as you'll discover in the book. Many letters have brought me close to tears, but just as many have made me chuckle. Apart from the romance, they're a marvellous insight into our social history. Even during the last six years I've seen a shift in attitude from listeners. Divorce seems to be much more tolerated now and the word partner has become totally accepted, whereas in the early days we'd be accused of encouraging people to live in sin!

If the programme has proved anything to me it's that romance is well and truly alive in the 1990s. And not just with the older generation. We get many letters from students who are going through the same emotional traumas as their grandparents did. Nostalgia is also doing well. One of the first letters I received was about a couple who were revisiting their honeymoon destination. The honeymoon had involved staying in a hut on a farm whilst strawberry picking. The bride had found a jam jar, put some dried flowers in it and placed it carefully on the shelf behind their camp-bed to celebrate their first night as man and wife. When they returned to the farm for the first time forty years later, not only was the hut still there but the improvised vase and flowers were still on the shelf.

Your letters were the inspiration for this anthology, but we've also included some famous love letters, romantic poetry and prose, and extracts from appropriate plays and films.

I hope you enjoy the book. *Classic Romance* has been so much part of my life that although I rarely meet the authors of the letters, I feel I know you all.

Nick Bailey

PROLOGUE

This listener's letter was included in the Classic Romance *programme of 17 October 1992 . . .*

KATE HARWOOD, LEEDS

Would you consider reading out a letter on your *Classic Romance* programme which doesn't really have a happy ending, although it is romantic?

Fourteen years ago, through a love of opera, I met the lovely man who became my husband. What joy to have a partner to share visits to operas, and listening and watching at home!

Our long-term plan was to visit Italy, where Frank had been stationed in the war, and to combine this with a visit to the Opera Festival at Verona – surely every opera-lover's dream!

Sadly, Frank became seriously ill, and after enduring this illness for a long while, he died in 1987. I now had to face life alone after only a few wonderful years. Needless to say this was a difficult time for me; I wasn't even forty yet, and already a widow!

The following year, I decided to take a holiday alone,

to come to terms with things, and at the same time fulfil our dream of going to Verona.

Sunday, 7 August found me in the beautiful amphitheatre in Rome; coincidentally this date was also our wedding anniversary. The opera was Puccini's *Turandot*, a favourite, and the performance was to begin at 9 p.m.

Imagine the wonder of it all when at 8.55 p.m. someone lit a candle, and the light was passed around, from person to person, as we all lit the three tiny candles we'd been given on entry. Now, as dusk fell, the arena glittered with the flickering of thousands of tiny candle flames – utter magic.

Silence fell, and the music began. I sat forward on my stone seat, rather apprehensive. This was after all an emotional moment for me.

Then, as the chorus went into 'Perché tarda la luna?' ('Why is the moon late?'), the hairs on the back of my neck began to prickle. The notes of this exquisite song seemed to float upwards into the velvet starlit sky and disperse into an unknown place, somewhere beyond time.

At that precise moment I felt a serenity, a knowledge that I *would* survive and life could be sweet again. I relaxed and revelled in the rest of that magical night.

Whenever, now, I hear that piece of music, I look back to that turning-point in my life and my determination to survive is strengthened.

PART ONE

First Encounters

VALENTINE

Wendy Cope (*b.* 1945)

My heart has made its mind up
And I'm afraid it's you.
Whatever you've got lined up,
My heart has made its mind up
And if you can't be signed up
This year, next year will do.
My heart has made its mind up
And I'm afraid it's you.

Before the First World War it was usually impossible to cross the rigid class barriers, but not for this couple.

Eric Matthews, Kinross

He was Fred — he came from a wealthy family and lived in a country house some miles out of town. There was also a town house in Kilmarnock. Each morning and evening he travelled by train between there and Irvine, a distance of some eight miles.

Her name was Martha — she lived in Irvine on the second floor of a tenement block the back garden of which abutted the railway line. Her father was a railway black-smith and she had seven sisters.

It was 1914 and they were both seventeen.

One early summer morning on the way to work, as the train slowed for Irvine station, he noticed an attractive girl looking out of the tenement window. It was the same the following morning, so on the third morning he couldn't resist waving to her through the open carriage window — hankie in hand, she waved back. This continued for a little while until Fred, by now deeply interested — she *was* very attractive — threw his morning paper down the embankment with a note inside which said 'My name is Fred'. She responded next morning by waving a bunch of flowers as she leaned out of her window.

The following week, by now completely intrigued, Fred dropped a bunch of carnations out of the carriage on to the embankment with a note saying 'Will you meet me on Saturday afternoon at 3 o'clock on the platform of Irvine station? If the answer is Yes, wave a hat from your window tomorrow morning.' Martha did wave with her biggest and brightest hat.

Thus the die was cast – they met as often as they could – but it was difficult since by this time Fred's father had heard of the possible existence of 'a very unsuitable young woman' and told his son in no uncertain terms that the relationship was to be discontinued immediately. Fred took little notice.

Early in 1916 he left his girl to go to war – they were not to meet for another three and a half years – by joining the Royal Artillery. His first stop was southern Ireland (then part of the UK) for intensive training before spending a year in Palestine, where Britain was fighting the Turks – then on to France via Italy.

At 3.50 a.m. on 31 July 1917 the Battle of Passchendaele, the most brutal of all the First War's brutal battles began. On 16 October, as the battle still went on, exhausted and shaking with fear as all soldiers were, Fred sent off a standard postcard with a shorthand note – 'Will you marry me?' Finally in November he received a reply – 'Yes, yes, sweetheart, but you have to come home first.'

Fred finally came home in October 1919.

He had had a word with the train driver, who stopped

just outside Irvine station and vigorously blew the whistle and continued to do so until Martha and her sisters appeared. They were together again.

They were incurable romantics, for on Valentine's Day 1920 they boarded the Irvine-to-Kilmarnock train where a diamond engagement ring was placed on Martha's third finger. Marriage followed in June 1921. Fred's father was not there.

In due course three children arrived, the middle one being the writer. It was a home full of love, laughter and music.

'She who has never lov'd, has never liv'd.'
John Gay (1685–1732)

OH, BLUSH NOT SO,
OH, BLUSH NOT SO

John Keats (1795–1821)

Oh, blush not so, oh, blush not so,
    Or I shall think ye knowing.
And if ye smile the blushing while,
    Then maidenheads are going.

There's a blush for won't, and a blush for shan't—
    And a blush for having done it.
There's a blush for thought, and a blush for naught,
    And a blush for just begun it.

Oh, sigh not so, oh, sigh not so,
    For it sounds of Eve's sweet pippin.
By those loosened hips you have tasted the pips
    And fought in an amorous nipping.

Will you play once more at nice-cut-core,
    For it only will last our youth out?
And we have the prime of the kissing time,
    We have not one sweet tooth out.

There's a sigh for yes, and a sigh for no,
    And a sigh for I can't bear it!
Oh, what can be done, shall we stay or run?
    Oh, cut the sweet apple and share it!

The pounding of the waves ... the surging of the music ... This just had to be the start of something big!

Heather Huey, Coleraine

It was Sunday, 1 January 1995. I drove to the nearby beach listening to *Classic Romance* on the radio and quietly hoping that 1995 would be a better year for me. Walking my dog on the beautiful Irish beach every Sunday was a great way to 'blow away the blues'.

I parked my car and admired the fantastic 'big' sea in front of me as the Atlantic sent huge waves crashing in on the beach. The music being played at that moment suited the sea – roaring and crashing – and I continued to listen as I put on my walking boots, gloves, etc.

I turned the ignition off and was surprised to hear the music still playing. I checked my radio – it was definitely off. Looking round, I spotted that the driver's window of a nearby car was open slightly, and it was from this car I could hear the music.

'Hi, do you also enjoy *Classic Romance*?' said a handsome man, and he smiled. He got out of his car, complete also with walking boots and a dog! We introduced ourselves, chatted and walked the entire length of the beach together, dogs frolicking in the surf near by.

Almost two years on we still walk on the beach, still

listen to Classic FM, and our relationship has gone from strength to strength.

'And Antony, who lost the world for love.'
John Dryden (1631–1700)

THE HILL

Rupert Brooke (1887–1915)

Although widely known and admired as a war poet, Rupert Brooke had already begun to establish his reputation with earlier works such as 'Grantchester' and 'The Great Lover'.

He fell in love with the fifteen-year-old Noel Olivier when she was still at Bedales School and he at Cambridge University: he sent this poem to her suggesting she should not read anything into it . . .

Breathless, we flung us on the windy hill,
    Laughed in the sun, and kissed the lovely grass.
    You said, 'Through glory and ecstasy we pass;
Wind, sun, and earth remain, the birds sing still,
When we are old, are old . . .' 'And when we die
All's over that is ours; and life burns on
Through other lovers, other lips,' said I,
'Heart of my heart, our heaven is now, is won!'

'We are Earth's best, that learnt her lesson here.
        Life is our cry. We have kept the faith!' we said;
        'We shall go down with unreluctant tread
Rose-crowned into the darkness!' ... Proud we were,
And laughed, that had such brave true things to say.
—And then you suddenly cried, and turned away.

RUPERT BROOKE TO
NOEL OLIVIER

Jan. 23–4. 1911

. . . Oh goddess, all the world lies about 'Nature' (a soiled word) except you & me. For you are of Earth, and (if not in words) say so: and I am not, & say I'm not. On the peaks no one but you shall live, you alone. And I, below, shall wait in a town, and meet you every month half way down the mountains, where the woods end.

. . . And that vision also fades, as less true than the other that puts us alone, above everything & everyone. Noel, we're equal and immortal and alone, and give and take as equals, & freely. I *can't* write. I wish I could tell you what we are. Oh we love & will love finelier than it has ever been done. Go out and take the splendid things of life, and clothe yourself in them, & crown yourself with them and we'll meet with all the world for a gift to each other. Damn you, read the truth that is under all this fustian I'm writing. You are more glorious than God: and I – Because you have taken me & kissed me the good outweighs all the evil there could possibly be and because we have kissed & you have, wonderfully, loved me (I don't only say with lips 'Noel', but every inch of me thrills & strains to you when I think the word) the world's an ecstasy, and there's no time to learn German or eat or do anything but sing. Read, and forgive, and glory. Noel, stranger, I, Rupert, am writing to you, I am afraid at the sound of your name, & of my own. Throw out arms across sea & lands to you. I love you.

Rupert

The music of Mozart and a broken cassette player brought this couple together.

BEATRICE ISHERWOOD, LONDON

Whilst travelling by train from London to Dover to visit an old school friend, I found myself sitting opposite a young man who settled down with his book and Walkman: obviously a seasoned traveller.

I spent my time gazing out of the window at the Kent countryside as I had not thought to bring any means of self-entertainment.

After a while the young man sitting opposite me started humming along to his tape. I listened to try and identify the tune and recognised it as the slow movement of Mozart's Clarinet Concerto.

This had been one of my favourite pieces since I had first heard it used in the film 'Out of Africa'.

Without thinking I too started humming the tune. Suddenly I realised that the young man had a problem with his Walkman and had switched it off leaving my lone voice warbling the beautifully haunting melody in the crowded carriage.

I immediately stopped and tried to hide my embarrassment by coughing and looking intently out of the window at the darkness of the tunnel we were passing through.

After I had composed myself I turned around and caught the young man looking at me. We both burst out laughing and struck up a conversation. It turned out that we had a lot more in common than just a love of Mozart's music. We were both organists in our local churches and also keen tennis players.

That was the beginning of our romance, and as happens, one thing led to another. We soon became engaged and are now married with two small children and will celebrate our fifth wedding anniversary in August.

'Love is like the measles; we all have to go through it.'
Jerome K. Jerome (1859–1927)

EUGÈNE DELACROIX
(1798–1863)
TO ELIZABETH SALTER

What makes this letter a labour of true love is the fact that the innovative French painter Delacroix needed frequent recourse to an English dictionary. On referring to the event at a later date, he said to a friend: 'I made up a wretched letter which will say things as best it can. I don't understand it too well myself and heaven knows if somebody else will . . .'

DECEMBER 1817

I not seen you E and you forget me absolutely. Often I have expected you and you have contemned my advertissements. I conceive you are wearied to see me in stairs to the face of the whole house, and I confess it not please me much. Yet, if we could understand we could find the means to frame even any swift moments. I not have lost memory of this happy evening when all babblers and troublesome were removed. You not remember probably last Friday;

but I have that present to my mind and I resent better for the want of so welcome occasion. Often, when I go near the kitchen I hear your fits of laughing, and I laugh in no wise. You ask me perhaps what matter is it to me. I will only answer such is my temper. Pardon me that caprice and my fantastical humour. I frame great many purposes to see you easily but needless ... I cannot call again to my mind that fortunate friday without a middle start of pleasure. The security of our company added over to the delight of your view. Oh my lips are arid, since had been cooled so deliciously. If my mouth could be so nimble to pronounce your linguage, as to savour so great sweetness, I not should be so wearied when I endeavour to speak or to write you. Pardon me if I call again to your memory the happiness which you have granted me. Not reproach me that, yet are so rare the Delights of Life. I beg you a favour: not refuse me. When Ch. L ... will be go out and when also L ... I conjure you make me known of that. Sometimes you will say it to me on the stairs: or if it not may be, you will have complaisance to say you have something to tell me: and I shall know what it signifies. You will not omit, you will tell me Sunday a thing which interest me. I am sure you laugh at it and you pepare to amuse me with trifflings. You are a cruel person which play afflicting the anothers. Nevertheless not be angry at it; I am a pitiful Englishman and I bet I have told in this write a multitude of impertinence, it must must therefore pardon me in consideration of my good intentions. Thought of me.

I will go out this evening. Prithee come a few. I hope God will remove ours enemies. I beg him for that. My whisker not sting more.

GREAT EXPECTATIONS

Charles Dickens (1812–1870)

As a shy and gauche young man, Pip is made to visit the eccentric Miss Havisham, who was jilted on her wedding night and has brought up her adopted niece Estella to hate men. Estella has learned her lesson well and, on their first encounter, treats Pip badly, unaware that her bitterness will eventually turn to love.

Miss Havisham beckoned her to come close, and took up a jewel from the table, and tried its effect upon her fair young bosom and against her pretty brown hair. 'Your own, one day, my dear, and you will use it well. Let me see you play cards with this boy.'

'With this boy! Why, he is a common labouring-boy!'

I thought I overheard Miss Havisham answer – only it seemed so unlikely – 'Well? You can break his heart.'

'What do you play, boy?' asked Estella of myself, with the greatest disdain.

'Nothing but beggar my neighbour, Miss.'

'Beggar him,' said Miss Havisham to Estella. So we sat down to cards . . .

'He calls the knaves, Jacks, this boy!' said Estella with disdain before our first game was out. 'And what coarse hands he has! And what thick boots!'

I had never thought of being ashamed of my hands before; but I began to consider them a very indifferent pair. Her contempt for me was so strong, that it became infectious, and I caught it.

She won the game, and I dealt. I misdealt, as was only natural, when I knew she was lying in wait for me to do wrong; and she denounced me for a stupid, clumsy labouring-boy.

'You say nothing of her,' remarked Miss Havisham to me, as she looked on. 'She says many hard things of you, yet you say nothing of her. What do you think of her?'

'I don't like to say,' I stammered.

'Tell me in my ear,' said Miss Havisham, bending down.

'I think she is very proud,' I replied, in a whisper.

'Anything else?'

'I think she is very pretty.'

'Anything else?'

'I think she is very insulting.' (She was looking at me then with a look of supreme aversion.)

'Anything else?'

'I think I should like to go home.'

'And never see her again, though she is so pretty?'

'I am not sure that I shouldn't like to see her again, but I should like to go home now.'

How would you feel if the man of your dreams was wearing a powdered wig and red stockings when you first met?

MARK WALLIS, GUILDFORD

My company recruits and trains people to work in historic sites in replica historic costume. When we first provided costumed guides at Hampton Court Palace, I was working in King William III's state apartments – in full splendour of powdered periwig, velvet suit, high heels, red stockings, ruffles and a sword.

Suddenly, a goddess, a vision, appeared before me! Not a ghost but a stunningly beautiful girl on holiday from Germany. This paragon stared intently at me and I realised that this was *the* profound moment of my life! She and I hesitated until her mother pushed her towards me for the obligatory photo. I took the chance to find out how long she was in England and tell her of an Elizabethan festival I was staging that weekend. She promised to come and my heart leapt!

On the day of the festival I was more nervous than usual, but she came, joined in the Elizabethan dancing with me, and – after a stolen kiss – flew back home. I was determined to marry her and at that moment resolved to write to her daily, sending flowers, poems, letters – anything so that she wouldn't forget me.

Well, my ruse worked! She wrote back incredible letters which showed that our interests in history, costume and music were identical. We fell completely in love and married a year later at her family's castle outside Munich.

'If this be not love, it is madness, and then it is pardonable.'
William Congreve (1670–1729)

SONNET FROM
THE PORTUGUESE XLIII

Elizabeth Barrett Browning (1806–1861)

How do I love thee? Let me count the ways.
I love thee to the depth and breadth and height
My soul can reach, when feeling out of sight
For the ends of Being and ideal Grace.
I love thee to the level of everyday's
Most quiet need, by sun and candlelight.
I love thee freely, as men strive for Right;
I love thee purely, as they turn from Praise.
I love thee with the passion put to use
In my old griefs, and with my childhood's faith.
I love thee with a love I seemed to lose
With my lost saints, – I love thee with the breath,
Smiles, tears, of all my life! – and, if God choose,
I shall but love thee better after death.

ROBERT BROWNING (1812–1889) TO ELIZABETH BARRETT (1806–1861)

Robert Browning was unsuccessful as a poet for many years and financially dependent on his family until he was well into his twenties.

Elizabeth Barrett suffered a spinal injury in childhood and, until her meeting with Browning, seemed doomed to seclusion from the world.

Their courtship under the eyes of her jealous, tyrannical father, their elopement and subsequent happy married life in Italy, are part of one of the most celebrated of all literary romances.

They met for the first time for months after Browning wrote this letter of admiration.

Friday 10 January 1845

I love your verses with all my heart, dear Miss Barrett, – and this is no offhand complimentary letter that I shall write, – whatever else, no prompt matter-of-course recognition of your genius and there a graceful and natural end of the thing: since the day last week when I first read your poems, I quite laugh to remember how I have been turning

31

and turning again in my mind what I should be able to tell you of their effect upon me — for in the first flush of delight I thought I would this once get out of my habit of purely passive enjoyment, when I do really enjoy, and thoroughly justify my admiration — perhaps even, as a loyal fellowcraftsman should, try and find fault and do you some little good to be proud of hereafter! — but nothing comes of it all — so into me has it gone, and part of me has it become, this great living poetry of yours, not a flower of which but took root and grew — oh, how different that is from lying to be dried and pressed flat and prized highly and put in a book with a proper account at top and bottom, and shut up and put away . . . and the book called a 'Flora', besides! After all I need not give up the thought of doing that, too, in time; because even now, talking with whoever is worthy, I can give a reason for my faith in one and another excellence, the fresh strange music, the affluent language, the exquisite pathos and true new brave thought — but in this addressing myself to you, your own self, and for the first time, my feeling rises altogether. I do, as I say, love these books with all my heart — and I love you too: do you know I was once not very far from seeing — really seeing you? Mr Kenyon said to me one morning would you like to see Miss Barrett? — then he went to announce me, — then he returned . . . you were too unwell — and now it is years ago — and I feel as at some untoward passage in my travels — as if I had been close, so close, to some world's-wonder in chapel or crypt, only a screen to push and I might have entered, but there was some slight ... so it now seems ... slight and just-sufficient bar to admission, and the half-opened door shut, and I went home my thousands of miles, and the sight was never to be!

Well, these Poems were to be — and this true thankful joy and pride with which I feel myself

Yours ever faithfully,
Robert Browning

With so many arrivals and departures, a railway station can often have bitter-sweet connotations for lovers. For our next letter-writer, it also became a nature reserve ...

CLIFF HARRISON, MANCHESTER

I was waiting to pick up a friend from a railway station when I noticed a most attractive girl. She suddenly stopped, gazed down at the pavement, then compelled others to make a detour. This lovely girl was standing guard over a slug until it reached the safety of the hedge. I was fascinated that such a beautiful girl was so caring and felt that I had to meet her.

I passed that station at the same time for many days but was disappointed. Then, weeks later, wonderfully, I saw my lovely slug-protector walking through Bolton, and, plucking up courage, I walked alongside her and asked, 'Have you saved any slugs lately?' Her surprise was accompanied by a burst of delightful laughter, and our instant affinity led us into an exhilarating evening and the discovery that we shared many interests.

Cupid comes in countless forms and that slug has accounted for many years of happy marriage.

'Alas! in truth the man but changed his mind
Perhaps was sick, in love, or had not dined.'
Alexander Pope (1688–1744)

THERE IS A LADY SWEET AND KIND

Anonymous (in Ford, Music of Sundry Kinds, 1607)

One fleeting glimpse of his beloved stranger put this unknown writer into an emotional turmoil.

But tomorrow, one suspects, may well be another day . . .

There is a lady sweet and kind,
Was never face so pleased my mind;
I did but see her passing by,
And yet I love her till I die.

Her gesture, motion, and her smiles,
Her wit, her voice, my heart beguiles,
Beguiles my heart, I know not why,
And yet I love her till I die.

Her free behaviour, winning looks,
Will make a lawyer burn his books;
I touched her not, alas! not I,
And yet I love her till I die.

Had I her fast betwixt mine arms,
Judge you that think such sports were harms,
Were't any harm? no, no, fie, fie,
For I will love her till I die.

Should I remain confinèd there
So long as Phoebus in his sphere,
I to request, she to deny,
Yet would I love her till I die.

Cupid is wingèd and doth range,
Her country so my love doth change:
But change she earth, or change she sky,
Yet will I love her till I die.

Beauty is, and always will be, in the eye of the beholder.

Elizabeth Morris, Chester

I was a beauty writer on a popular women's magazine. My editor told me to have a facial at a Bond Street beauty salon and write it up in detail for the beauty page.

I emerged from the salon, my rosy cheeks completely camouflaged, pale and interesting for the first time in my life. By now it was late afternoon and I went straight on to a cocktail party where I met the man who has been my husband for twenty-nine years. However, I always feel I gained his love under false pretences because never since our first meeting has he again seen the pale and interesting face he fell for. The salon's technique was beyond my skills to do other than write about it!

When the article was published my editor inserted a PS at the end to this effect: '*Immediately after receiving this beauty treatment our beauty writer met the man who is now her fiancé.*' Later, no fewer than sixty readers got in touch with the Bond Street salon to ask for the very same beauty treatment which led to my romance.

'*Love ceases to be a pleasure, when it ceases to be a secret.*'
Aphra Behn (1640–1689)

THE IMPORTANCE OF
BEING EARNEST

Oscar Wilde (1854–1900)

Oscar Wilde wrote The Importance of Being Earnest *at a time when the corrupting influence of a naked table leg was best hidden from view. Given the moral correctness of that age, the behaviour of Jack and Gwendolen at such an early stage of their relationship is positively indecent.*

JACK: Charming day it has been, Miss Fairfax.

GWENDOLEN: Pray don't talk to me about the weather, Mr Worthing. Whenever people talk to me about the weather, I always feel quite certain that they mean something else. And that makes me so nervous.

JACK: I do mean something else.

GWENDOLEN: I thought so. In fact, I am never wrong.

JACK: And I would like to be allowed to take advantage of Lady Bracknell's temporary absence . . .

GWENDOLEN: I would certainly advise you to do so. Mamma has a way of coming back suddenly into a room that I have often had to speak to her about.

JACK (*nervously*): Miss Fairfax, ever since I met you I have admired you more than any girl ... I have ever met since ... I met you.

GWENDOLEN: Yes, I am quite well aware of the fact. And I often wish that in public, at any rate, you had been more demonstrative. For me you have always had an irresistible fascination. Even before I met you I was far from indifferent to you. (JACK *looks at her in amazement*) We live, as I hope you know, Mr Worthing, in an age of ideals. The fact is constantly mentioned in the more expensive monthly magazines, and has now reached the provincial pulpits, I am told; and my ideal has always been to love some one of the name of Ernest. There is something in that name that inspires absolute confidence. The moment Algernon first mentioned to me that he had a friend called Ernest, I knew I was destined to love you. The name, fortunately for my peace of mind, is, as far as my own experience goes, extremely rare.

JACK: You really love me, Gwendolen?

GWENDOLEN: Passionately!

JACK: Darling! You don't know how happy you've made me.

GWENDOLEN: My own Ernest! (*They embrace*)

JACK: But you don't really mean to say that you couldn't love me if my name wasn't Ernest?

GWENDOLEN: But your name is Ernest.

JACK: Yes, I know it is. But supposing it was something else. Do you mean to say you couldn't love me then?

GWENDOLEN (*glibly*): Ah! that is clearly a metaphysical speculation, and like most metaphysical speculations has very little reference at all to the actual facts of real life, as we know them.

JACK: Personally, darling, to speak quite candidly, I don't much care about the name of Ernest ... I don't think the name suits me at all.

GWENDOLEN: It suits you perfectly. It is a divine name. It has a music of its own. It produces vibrations.

JACK: Well, really, Gwendolen, I must say that I think there are lots of other much nicer names. I think Jack, for instance, a charming name.

GWENDOLEN: Jack? ... No, there is very little music in the name Jack, if any at all, indeed. It does not thrill. It produces absolutely no vibrations ... I have known several Jacks, and they all, without exception, were more than usually plain. Besides, Jack is a notorious domesticity for John! And I pity any woman who is married to a man called John. She would have a very tedious life with him. She would probably never be allowed to know the entrancing pleasure of a single moment's solitude. The only really safe name is Ernest.

JACK: Gwendolen, I must get christened at once – I mean we must get married at once. There is no time to be lost.

GWENDOLEN: Married, Mr Worthing?

JACK (*astounded*): Well . . . surely. You know that I love you, and you led me to believe, Miss Fairfax, that you were not absolutely indifferent to me.

GWENDOLEN: I adore you. But you haven't proposed to me yet. Nothing has been said at all about marriage. The subject has not even been touched on.

JACK: Well . . . may I propose to you now?

GWENDOLEN: I think it would be an admirable opportunity. And to spare you any possible disappointment, Mr Worthing, I think it only fair to tell you quite frankly beforehand that I am fully determined to accept you.

JACK: Gwendolen!

GWENDOLEN: Yes, Mr Worthing, what have you got to say to me?

JACK: You know what I have got to say to you.

GWENDOLEN: Yes, but you don't say it.

JACK: Gwendolen, will you marry me? (*Goes on his knees.*)

GWENDOLEN: Of course I will, darling. How long you have been about it! I am afraid you have had very little experience in how to propose.

JACK: My own one, I have never loved anyone in the world but you.

GWENDOLEN: Yes, but men often propose for practice. I know my brother Gerald does. All my girl-friends tell me so. What wonderfully blue eyes you have, Ernest! They are quite, quite blue. I hope you will always look at me just like that, especially when there are other people present.

TO CELIA

Ben Jonson (1572–1637)

*Ben Jonson's first original play – Every Man in his Humour –
was performed in 1598 with a young actor called William Shakespeare in
the cast. 'To Celia' is probably his best-known poem and was published
in the first folio of 1616.*

Drinke to me, onely, with thine eyes,
    And I will pledge with mine;
Or leave a kisse but in the cup,
    And I'll not look for wine.
The thirst that from the soule doth rise,
    Doth aske a drink divine:
But might I of Jove's nectar sup,
    I would not change for thine.
I sent thee, late, a rosie wreath,
    Not so much honouring thee,
As giving it a hope, that there

It could not withered bee.
But thou thereon did'st onely breath,
    And sent'st it backe to me:
Since when it growes, and smells, I sweare,
    Not of it selfe, but thee.

Not many paying guests offer to tackle the garden. Even fewer stay on to see how it will grow ...

SHEILA NAISH, HEBDEN BRIDGE

I run a small B&B in West Yorkshire, and met Joe when he booked in for an overnight stay, *by mistake ...*

He'd got the phone numbers muddled and really wanted Vine Cottage, where he'd stayed before. But having realised his error over the booking he was too polite, or too embarrassed, to go back on the arrangement.

He arrived on a November evening. I opened the door to admit: one plastic bag, overstrained; a paper bag of Bramleys teetering at the top; one elderly khaki canvas haversack, greasy and fraying; one sagging green corduroy jacket, pockets bursting; one green beret set at a jaunty angle. Smoky November dusk followed him into the room and hung around that jacket, but he swept off the beret with an air. Standing at that chilly doorstep I nevertheless felt warm.

Next morning he was just about to pay the bill when an idea seemed to strike him. 'Your garden needs doing,' he said. 'I'm at a loose end.'

This is how we began. About six months later Joe moved in with me. He has transformed the garden. Whether we have transformed each other, or have remained obstinately unchanged, is another tale, but we're still here, and love grows.

'Is it not a fashion for the maids in France to kiss before they are married?'
William Shakespeare, Henry V

LEOŠ JANÁČEK (1854–1928) TO KAMILA STOSSLOVA (1892–1935)

At the age of sixty-three, the composer Leoš Janáček fell in love with the wife of an antique dealer and wrote to her almost every day — nearly seven hundred times altogether. Here is one of his earliest letters.

Luhacovice
16th July 1917

Madam,

Please accept these few roses as proof of how greatly I hold you in esteem. Your personality and appearance are so pleasing that one feels lighthearted in your company; you breathe such sincerity and regard the world with such kindness, that one wants also to repay you only by goodness and kindness. You have no idea how pleased I am to have met you.

You lucky one! The more painfully do I feel my own loneliness and harsh fate.

Think of me always with kindness – that's how you will remain in my thoughts for ever.

Your sincerely devoted,
Leoš Janáček

Anonymous

(in John Dowland's *First Book of Songs or Airs*, 1597)

Dear, if you change, I'll never choose again;
Sweet, if you shrink, I'll never think of love;
Fair, if you fail, I'll judge all beauty vain;
Wise, if too weak, more wits I'll never prove.
    Dear, sweet, fair, wise, change, shrink, nor be not weak;
    And, on my faith, my faith shall never break.

Earth with her flowers shall sooner heaven adorn;
Heaven her bright stars, through earth's dim globe shall move.
Fire, heat shall lose; and frosts of flames be born;
Air made to shine, as black as hell shall prove:
    Earth, heaven, fire, air, the world transformed shall view,
    Ere I prove false to faith, or strange to you.

PART TWO

True Romance

TO MY DEAR AND LOVING HUSBAND

Anne Bradstreet (1612–1672)

Anne Bradstreet was an English-born poet of the Massachusetts Bay Colony, although her verse reveals a sensitivity to love and beauty not normally associated with the Puritans.

If ever two were one, then surely we.
If ever man were lov'd by wife, then thee;
If ever wife was happy in a man,
Compare with me ye women if you can.
I prize thy love more than whole Mines of gold,
Or all the riches that the East doth hold.
My love is such that Rivers cannot quench,
Nor ought but love from thee, give recompence.
Thy love is such I can no way repay,
The heavens reward thee manifold I pray.
Then while we live, in love lets so persever,
That when we live no more, we may live ever.

Even wartime bombs could not stop the beginning of more than fifty years of romance.

MARIE WRIGHT, BRISTOL

On 14 November 1940, like many other cities, Coventry was badly bombed. My wedding to Bill was planned for 30 November – St Andrew's Day. Coming from a totally Scottish background, despite the difficulties, I was determined the wedding should go ahead on this date.

The first setback was the photographer, whose studio was flattened, but he promised to do his best in a darkened garden hut.

The second problem was that the restaurant booked for the reception was also bombed, but a few tins of ham and fruit were salvaged, and my mother said she would do her best at home.

By now the guest list was reduced by our large number of Scottish relatives and friends declining to come to Coventry.

The best man and bridesmaid arrived in a borrowed car and took Mother off to the church. Father and I sat and waited for our taxi – and waited – and waited. I was thinking of walking two miles in my finery – when the taxi came. 'Sorry, my dear,' the driver said, 'every road I tried was closed with a big notice, "UNEXPLODED BOMB"!'

So we got to church – the vicar was standing in the porch, no music. 'Sorry,' he said, 'the organ was badly damaged last night when all the windows were blown out.' The guests, what few there were, were frozen, but the poor groom was whiter than white and quite convinced I had changed my mind.

What a day – but here we are, fifty-three years on, and happy together counting our blessings, and looking forward to our Diamond Wedding, obviously great survivors just like the City of Coventry.

'God is love, I dare say. But what a mischievous devil love is.'
Samuel Butler (1835–1902)

THE INDIAN SERENADE

Percy Bysshe Shelley (1792–1822)

I arise from dreams of thee
In the first sweet sleep of night.
When the winds are breathing low,
And the stars are shining bright:
I arise from dreams of thee,
And a spirit in my feet
Hath led me – who knows how?
To thy chamber window, Sweet!

The wandering airs they faint
On the dark, the silent stream—
The Champak odours fail
Like sweet thoughts in a dream;
The nightingale's complaint,
It dies upon her heart;—
As I must on thine,
Oh, belovèd as thou art!

Oh lift me from the grass!
I die! I faint! I fail!
Let thy love in kisses rain
On my lips and eyelids pale.
My cheek is cold and white, alas!
My heart beats loud and fast;—
Oh! press it to thine own again,
Where it will break at last.

ALBAN BERG (1885–1935) TO HELENE NAHOWSKI

How should a wife react when she finds 'the other woman' is Mahler's Third Symphony?

This letter was written by the Austrian composer Alban Berg to his wife, Helène.

Vienna

Today, my darling, I have been unfaithful to you for the first time. You know, of course, that my idea of fidelity is different from most people's. For me it means a state of mind which never leaves the lover, follows him like a shadow and grows into part of his personality: the feeling that he is never alone, always dependent on another, that without the beloved he is no longer a whole person capable of sustaining life.

It was in this sense I was unfaithful to you tonight. It happened in the finale of the Mahler symphony (No. 3), when I gradually felt a sensation of complete solitude, as if in all the world there were nothing left but this music – and me listening to it. But when it came to its uplifting and overwhelming climax, and then was over, I felt a sudden pang, and a voice within me said: what of Helene? It was only then I realized I had been unfaithful, so now I implore your forgiveness. Tell me, darling, that you understand and forgive!

After Berg's death, his wife wrote 'For eighty years I lived in the paradise of his love'.

SONNET No. 38

William Shakespeare (1564–1616)

How can my muse want subject to invent
While thou dost breathe, that pour'st into my verse
Thine own sweet argument, too excellent
For every vulgar paper to rehearse?
O, give thyself the thanks if aught in me
Worthy perusal stand against thy sight;
For who's so dumb that cannot write to thee,
When thou thyself dost give invention light?
Be thou the tenth muse, ten times more in worth
Than those old nine which rhymers invocate,
And he that calls on thee, let him bring forth
Eternal numbers to outlive long date.
    If my slight muse do please these curious days,
    The pain be mine, but thine shall be the praise.

Real romance — the sort that will stand the test of a lifetime — can sneak up when you least expect it.

WINNIE JONES, LLANGADOG

Some six years ago, when I was in my late twenties, I felt very much in an emotional quandary, swept up in the enjoyment of an exciting career with a London PR firm but missing the Great Outdoors — so much so that I seemed to be spending more and more time at my parents' home in the country and generally beginning to wonder what life really did have in store for me.

One winter's evening, on one of my frequent visits home, I arranged to accept a lift from a young hill farmer as we'd both been invited to spend a few hours at the home of mutual friends, also hill farmers. As the evening progressed in a happy and jovial atmosphere, I looked across at my driver for the evening and saw just the most wonderful and warm person I had ever met in my life.

A feeling of total panic gripped me as we left for home because I realised that, once this marvellous man had dropped me off, I would probably never see him again. I thanked my farmer for the lift and wished him goodnight, but as my feet touched the ground, I went flying! I had been totally unaware of the liberal covering of black ice over South Wales that night.

What was only meant to be a short time alone in each other's company became an all-nighter – in the casualty department of the nearest hospital. I was in hospital for a week, but my farmer friend didn't turn up until the last night. There he was – he had some business in the area and really felt he ought to pop in and see me for five minutes! Five minutes soon became long in-depth conversations and we felt we'd known each other for years.

Well, I married my farmer and we have been blessed with two beautiful children, a daughter who is three and a son of fourteen months. We lead a close and wonderful family life with a lot of hard work and a lot of laughter, farming sheep on a blustery Welsh hillside.

'It's love, it's love that makes the world go round.'
French popular song

STELLA'S BIRTHDAY

Jonathan Swift (1667–1745)

Esther Johnson was immortalised by Jonathan Swift in his Jour-nal to Stella. Their friendship began in 1689 and lasted until her death in 1728.

Written in the Year 1718

Stella this day is thirty-four,
(We shan't dispute a year or more:)
However Stella, be not troubled,
Although thy size and years are doubled,
Since first I saw thee at sixteen,
The brightest virgin on the green.
So little is thy form declined;
Made up so largely in thy mind.

Oh, would it please the gods to *split*
Thy beauty, size, and years, and wit,
No age could furnish out a pair

Of nymphs so graceful, wise and fair:
With half the lustre of your eyes,
With half your wit, your years, and size:
And then before it grew too late,
How should I beg of gentle fate,
(That neither nymph might have her swain,)
To split my worship too in twain.

HENRI OF NAVARRE
(1553–1610) TO
GABRIELLE D'ESTRÉES

Gabrielle d'Estrées won the affection of the King of Navarre when he visited her father's castle at Coeuvres in northern France. She became his mistress and bore him several children, all of whom were legitimised.

Navarre, first of the Bourbon dynasty, had planned to marry her, but she died before he was able to divorce Margaret of Valois.

10 February 1593

I know not with what magic you have wrought, heart of my heart, but I never endured other severances with half the impatience the present one inflicts on me. Already it seems an age since I departed from you. No need for you to beg me to return. Every artery, every muscle in my body keeps telling me, every moment, of the bliss of beholding you and of the bitterness of separation. Believe me, my beloved Queen, never did love visit me so fiercely as it does this very hour. I kiss your beautiful hands a million times.

17 February 1593

The pain I feel at getting no news from you continues still. I am sending La Fon to you poste-haste for I fear some accident must have befallen you. Send him back at once, dear love, I implore you. Believe me, my lovely angel, when I say that I rate the possession of your good graces above the glory of a dozen battles. Consider it a jewel in your crown that you have vanquished me, who never was completely conquered save by you, whose feet I kiss a million times.

So often children are much more perceptive than their parents . . .

FRANCES LAWRENCE, GREAT BOOKHAM

I was a single parent with a little boy. Life had been difficult at times, but James and I were very happy together.

One Christmas I asked James what we should put on his list to Father Christmas. He replied 'a daddy' and the tears streamed down my face.

I started a new job later that year, and became friendly with a girl who told me she worked with someone I should meet. I could see she was scheming and wasn't too keen to play along as I was quite happy alone. All her attempts to introduce Peter and I failed as he was never where she said he would be. Eventually we all went out to lunch at a Chinese restaurant. Peter was quite shy and didn't say much, so I could not form any opinion about him. My friend told me Peter would be going to the works Christmas party. Don't ask me why, but I bought a horrendously expensive designer dress and went to the party but guess what – Peter didn't go. I was livid and determined to get closer now that he didn't seem interested. For months he avoided me until we were at the same sales conference and I, fortified by wine, asked him out.

We began going out, and Peter was very understanding with James and never moaned when we hardly every were able to go out alone, and certainly could not have a weekend together. Eventually Peter asked me to marry him, but I refused as I was not sure James would want another man taking his place in my affections.

Peter and I continued our romance, and I think he wondered at times if there was any point. He asked me to marry him, and again I said no. We decided to book a holiday to St Lucia, just the three of us! Peter said they performed weddings there and I said I knew that, and was sure it must be very nice but *we* wouldn't be one of the weddings.

One day, before we went, I was sitting on the bottom of the stairs putting on James's shoes ready for school, when he casually looked at me and said 'I don't know why you and Peter don't get married.' I was dumbfounded and asked him if that was all right, and he said it was fine. So in August 1993 Peter and I were married in St Lucia with James as best man. Peter has since adopted James, and we now have a 3 year old son of our own. Life is wonderful, and we still have never had the time away alone together.

THE CONFIRMATION

Edwin Muir (1887–1959)

Yes, yours, my love, is the right human face.
I in my mind had waited for this long,
Seeing the false and searching for the true,
Then found you as a traveller finds a place
Of welcome suddenly amid the wrong
Valleys and rocks and twisting roads. But you,
What shall I call you? A fountain in a waste,
A well of water in a country dry,
Or anything that's honest and good, an eye
That makes the whole world bright. Your open heart,
Simple with giving, gives the primal deed,
The first good world, the blossom, the blowing seed,
The hearth, the steadfast land, the wandering sea.
Not beautiful or rare in every part.
But like yourself, as they were meant to be.

JAMAICA INN

Daphne du Maurier (1907–1989)

Jem Merlyn is a good-for-nothing horse thief, liable to be arrested and hanged at any time. The future he offers Mary Yellan – heroine of Jamaica Inn *– is insecure, uncertain and full of hardship. Will she take that risk?*

He took her face in his hands and kissed it, and she saw that he was laughing. 'When you're an old maid in mittens down at Helford, you'll remember that,' he said, 'and it will have to last you to the end of your days. "He stole horses," you'll say to yourself, "and he didn't care for women; and but for my pride I'd have been with him now."'

He climbed into the cart and looked down upon her, flicking his whip and yawning. 'I'll do fifty miles before tonight,' he said, 'and sleep like a puppy at the end of it, in a tent by the side of the road. I'll kindle a fire, and cook bacon for my supper. Will you think of me, or not?'

She did not listen, though; she stood with her face towards the south, hesitating and twisting her hands. Beyond those hills the bleak moors turned to pasture, and the pasture to valleys and to streams. The peace and quiet of Helford waited for her beside the running water.

'It's not pride,' she told him; 'you know that it's not pride; there's a sickness in my heart for home and all the things I've lost.'

He said nothing, but drew the reins into his hands and whistled to the horse. 'Wait,' said Mary, 'wait, and hold him still, and give me your hand.'

He laid the whip aside, and reached down to her, and swung her beside him on the driver's seat.

'What now?' he said. 'And where do you want me to take you? You have your back to Helford, do you know that?'

'Yes, I know,' she said.

'If you come with me it will be a hard life, and a wild one at times, Mary, with no biding anywhere, and little rest and comfort. Men are ill companions when the mood takes them, and I, God knows, the worst of them. You'll get a poor exchange for your farm, and small prospect of the peace you crave.'

'I'll take the risk, Jem, and chance your moods.'

'Do you love me, Mary?'

'I believe so, Jem.'

'Better than Helford?'

'I can't ever answer that.'

'Why are you sitting here beside me, then?'

'Because I want to; because I must; because now and for evermore this is where I long to be,' said Mary.

He laughed then, and took her hand, and gave her the reins; and she did not look back over her shoulder again, but set her face towards the Tamar.

A SUBALTERN'S LOVE-SONG

Sir John Betjeman (1906–1984)

Miss J. Hunter Dunn, Miss J. Hunter Dunn,
Furnish'd and burnish'd by Aldershot sun,
What strenuous singles we played after tea,
We in the tournament – you against me!

Love-thirty, love-forty, oh! weakness of joy,
The speed of a swallow, the grace of a boy,
With carefullest carelessness, gaily you won,
I am weak from your loveliness, Joan Hunter Dunn.

Miss Joan Hunter Dunn, Miss Joan Hunter Dunn,
How mad I am, sad I am, glad that you won.
The warm-handled racket is back in its press,
But my shock-headed victor, she loves me no less.

Her father's euonymus shines as we walk,
And swing past the summer-house, buried in talk,
And cool the verandah that welcomes us in
To the six-o'clock news and a lime-juice and gin.

The scent of the conifers, sound of the bath,
The view from my bedroom of moss-dappled path,
As I struggle with double-end evening tie,
For we dance at the Golf Club, my victor and I.

On the floor of her bedroom lie blazer and shorts
And the cream-coloured walls are be-trophied with sports,
And westering, questioning settles the sun
On your low-leaded window, Miss Joan Hunter Dunn.

The Hillman is waiting, the light's in the hall,
The pictures of Egypt are bright on the wall,
My sweet, I am standing beside the oak stair
And there on the landing's the light on your hair.

By roads not 'adopted', by woodlanded ways,
She drove to the club in the late summer haze,
Into nine-o'clock Camberley, heavy with bells
And mushroomy, pine-woody, evergreen smells.

Miss Joan Hunter Dunn, Miss Joan Hunter Dunn,
I can hear from the car-park the dance has begun.
Oh! full Surrey twilight! importunate band!
Oh! strongly adorable tennis-girl's hand!

Around us are Rovers and Austins afar,
Above us, the intimate roof of the car,
And here on my right is the girl of my choice,
With the tilt of her nose and the chime of her voice,

And the scent of her wrap, and the words never said,
And the ominous, ominous dancing ahead.
We sat in the car-park till twenty to one
And now I'm engaged to Miss Joan Hunter Dunn.

Love letters in the sand?
The writing surface may have been different, but the sentiments
were the same.

PATRICK MOORE, SOUTHAMPTON

In November 1981, as a widowed father of two small daughters, I met Fiona, the niece of a fellow naval officer and also a single parent with her own daughter. I was shore-based at that time and Fiona and I became good friends. I asked Fiona if she would be prepared to live in my house with our daughters while I was at sea and to my surprise she agreed.

My ship was duly sent to the South Atlantic on a five-month Falklands patrol. Fiona wrote every day and I always felt close to home with her letters and diary tapes. Once a month we would come into Port Stanley for a few days and, like many others, I would savour precious moments telephoning home. Each time I felt more and more for the lady taking such good care of our family.

With two months to go we were sent to the remote island of South Georgia. It was one of the most memorable trips of my naval career. The towering glaciers and huge icebergs were awesome. The dangerous beauty of ice six inches thick on the ship decks in glorious southern sunshine, coupled with an overpowering stillness and peace, is a memory which still fills me with wonder. I was able to get ashore for a while and visit the now-deserted whaling station. I climbed the snow-clad hill to see the old church where Shackleton had been buried in 1922. The surrounding silence was eerie and humbling in nature.

In this solitude, I began to wonder what life had in store on my return to England. It was then that I decided that I should share my life with Fiona. In a mad moment I carved her name in the snow in huge letters and signed it with love. A colleague indulged me and took the photographs for posterity. Needless to say, when Fiona saw the photographs, the bond between us became stronger. That evening my captain dined in the officers' mess. He had been up in the helicopter and asked who had a lady friend by the name of Fiona. He had seen my declaration of love from the air and thought that the message would last, etched in the ice, at least until the end of the southern summer. I flushed in awkward silence, but in those days moments such as these were understood by everyone.

Eventually my ship returned home to Fiona and the girls. I was more convinced that my experience in South Georgia had directed my destiny. We married in February 1985 and now have four wonderful daughters between us. I would dearly love to take Fiona back to South Georgia and one day that may happen. In the meantime we are planning an Alaskan cruise, on which we can share the power and majesty of snow-covered mountains and glaciers as well as their peace and solitude.

'When beauty fires the blood, how love exalts the mind.'
John Dryden (1631–1700)

JOHN ANDERSON

Robert Burns (1759–1796)

John Anderson my jo, John,
    When we were first acquent;
Your locks were like the raven,
    Your bonnie brow was brent;
But now your brow is beld, John,
    Your locks are like the snow;
But blessings on your frosty pow,
    John Anderson, my jo.

John Anderson my jo, John,
    We clamb the hill thegither;
And mony a canty day, John,
    We've had wi' ane anither:
Now we maun totter down, John,
    And hand in hand we'll go;
And sleep thegither at the foot,
    John Anderson, my jo.

'Jo' can mean joy or pleasure as well as a sweetheart or beloved one.

ELIZABETH LINLEY
(1754–1792) TO RICHARD BRINSLEY SHERIDAN
(1751–1816)

Having achieved fame as a public performer, the singer Elizabeth Linley was the target of countless sexual propositions. Richard Sheridan, the future playwright, became her champion and protector and, before they were married in 1773, he corresponded with her secretly, helped her escape to France, and fought two duels in defence of her honour.

11 o'clock

Though I parted from you so lately, and though I expect to see you again so soon, yet I cannot keep my fingers from the pen but I must be plaguing you with my scrawl. Oh, my dearest love, I am never happy but when I am with you. I cannot speak or think of anything else. When shall we have another happy half hour? I declare I have not felt real joy since I came from France before this evening. Perhaps now while I am writing and amusing myself by expressing the tender sentiments which I feel for you, you are flirting with Miss W, or some other handsome girl . . .

I really think Charles suspected something this evening. He looked amazingly knowing when I came down. Deuce take his curious head. I wish he would mind his own business and not interrupt us in our stolen pleasures. Is it not amazing, my dear Love, that we should always have so great an inclination for what is not in our possession? . . .

Let me see, what have I more to say? – nothing but the same dull story over and over again – that I love you to distraction, and that I would prefer you and beggary before any other man and a throne. I will call you Horatio – that was the name you gave yourself in that sweet poem – write to me then, my dear Horatio, and tell me that you are equally sincere and constant . . .

My hand shakes so I can scarce hold the pen. My father came into my room this moment, and I had just time to stuff the letter behind the glass. 'Twas well he did not take much notice of me, for I was . . . Goodbye. God bless – I will . . .

THE GOOD-MORROW

John Donne (1572–1631)

John Donne's love poetry is remarkable for the depth of its analysis of the nature and psychology of love — unlike the conventional courtly verse of his day.

I wonder by my troth, what thou, and I
Did, till we lov'd? were we not wean'd till then?
But suck'd on countrey pleasures, childishly?
Or snorted we in the seven sleepers' den?
'Twas so; but this, all pleasures fancies bee;
If ever any beauty I did see,
Which I desir'd, and got, 'twas but a dreame of thee.

And now good morrow to our waking soules,
Which watch not one another out of feare;
For love, all love of other sights controules,
And makes one little roome an every where.
Let sea-discoverers to new worlds have gone,

Let maps to other, worlds on worlds have showne,
Let us possesse one world, each hath one, and is one.

My face in thine eye, thine in mine appeares,
And true plaine hearts doe in the faces rest,
Where can we finde two better hemispheares
Without sharpe North, without declining West?
What ever dyes, was not mixt equally;
If our two loves be one, or thou and I
Love so alike, that none doe slacken, none can die.

A tale of two cities …

JENNY TUDOR, ISLE OF WIGHT

This is really two love stories – involving the same man.

It is 1879. George is now twenty-three, a good-looking young man who has finished his studies. There is no rush to find any gainful employment as his family is wealthy, having made their money from shipbuilding in North Yorkshire where they live in a beautiful house, with servants to wait upon them. In any case, George is not the stuff of which Yorkshire businessmen are made – being a romantic young man with an artistic streak!

He falls desperately in love with Mary, a very pretty scullery maid who is twenty-two. They meet secretly as the family obviously would not approve of such a romance. Shortly afterwards Mary becomes pregnant and they run off to London where they marry in secret. Surprisingly, the family do not cut him off without a penny and he continues to receive his 'allowance' from the family business. The years pass, and Mary goes on to bear him eleven more children. As time goes on, George finds his lifestyle more and more restricting, and one day he disappears from home. To their credit, the family continue to support Mary, who brings up the children despite increasingly poor sight and health.

George, meanwhile, has fled to Paris to fulfil a long-cherished dream to become an artist. There he meets a kindred spirit – a Frenchwoman, also an artist, and they set up home together. He has moderate success as an artist but it doesn't really matter as he still has his 'allowance' to live on and he has found the understanding and love of a woman who appreciates his talents. They live happily together until George dies, aged eighty-four, the day before the Germans invade Paris in 1940.

Of the twelve children born to George and Mary, only one, Winifred, married. Winifred was my grandmother and I can remember going to see Mary (or 'Ummy', as we called her) when I was very young and we were evacuated to Yorkshire during the war. By then she was a very frail old lady who was completely blind, but her beauty shone through even at that age. She died in 1944. I regret to say that I never met my great-grandfather, who must have been quite a character.

One of my earliest and happiest memories is of my grandmother playing 'The Merry Widow' and other delights on the piano (by ear, as she had never had a lesson in her life), with Ummy sitting in her chair, listening, with a beautiful smile on her face.

'This maiden she lived with no other thought
Than to love and be loved by me.'
Edgar Allan Poe (1809–1849)

SHE WALKS IN BEAUTY

George Gordon, Lord Byron (1788–1824)

The poet Byron was one of the greatest of all romantics. This poem was inspired by the sight of his cousin, Mrs Wilmot, wearing a beautiful evening gown.

She walks in beauty, like the night
    Of cloudless climes and starry skies;
And all that's best of dark and bright
    Meet in her aspect and her eyes:
Thus mellowed to that tender light
    Which heaven to gaudy day denies.

One shade the more, one ray the less,
    Had half impaired the nameless grace
Which waves in every raven tress
    Or softly lightens o'er her face;
Where thoughts serenely sweet express
    How pure, how dear their dwelling-place.

And on that cheek, and o'er that brow,
    So soft, so calm, yet eloquent,
The smiles that win, the tints that glow,
    But tell of days in goodness spent,
A mind at peace with all below,
    A heart whose love is innocent.

UPON THE DEATH OF SIR ALBERT MORTON'S WIFE

Sir Henry Wotton (1568–1639)

Sir Henry Wotton was a very interesting character. A lawyer who became a spy, he coined the phrase, 'An Ambassador is an honest man sent to lie abroad for his country.' His published work includes the intriguing title, 'On his mistress, the Queen of Bohemia'.

He first deceased; she for a little tried
To live without him, liked it not, and died.

THE CONSTANT LOVER

John Suckling (1609–1642)

Sir John Suckling was well known for his wit, gaiety, extravagance and love of gaming. He was implicated in a plot to rescue the Earl of Strafford from the Tower of London in 1641, and was forced to flee to France, where he died the following year.

Out upon it, I have lov'd
 Three whole days together!
And am like to love three more,
 If it hold fair weather.

Time shall moult away his wings
 Ere he shall discover
In the whole wide world again
 Such a constant lover.

But a pox upon't, no praise
    There is due at all to me:
Love with me had made no stay,
    Had it any been but she.

Had it any been but she,
    And that very very face,
There had been at least ere this
    A dozen dozen in her place.

PART THREE

What Might Have Been

LOVE'S SECRET

William Blake (1757–1827)

Never seek to tell thy love,
    Love that never told can be;
For the gentle wind does move
    Silently, invisibly.

I told my love, I told my love,
    I told her all my heart,
Trembling, cold, in ghastly fears—
    Ah, she doth depart.

Soon as she was gone from me,
    A traveller came by
Silently, invisibly—
    O, was no deny.

HANS VON BULOW
(1830–1894) TO COSIMA
VON BULOW

Cosima, the daughter of Franz Liszt, had two children by Richard Wagner before she divorced the writer of this letter, her husband, the conductor and pianist Hans von Bulow.

   Between the lines of the following letter must surely be found the most profound regret for a lost love.

Munich
17 June 1869

I am grateful to you, dear Cosima, for having taken the initiative and shall give you no reason to regret it. I am indeed too unhappy myself – through my own fault – not to wish to avoid wounding you by any unjust reproach whatsoever. As regards this most painful separation, which you have felt to be necessary, I recognise all the wrongs on my side and shall continue to lay stress on them in the inevitable discussion on the matter with my mother and your father. I have made you poor, a sorry return for all the great kindness you have lavished upon me in our past life. Your own existence was poisoned by me and I can only thank providence for having offered you some compensation, however inadequate, at almost the last moment, when courage to go on shouldering your burden must have been failing you. But, alas, since you left me, I have lost my sole support in life and in my struggle. It was your mind, your heart, your patience, indulgence, sympathy, encouragement, and advice – last and most especially, your presence, your face, and your speech – which, taken all together, constituted that support. The loss of this supreme good, whose full value I recognise only after its loss, has brought about moral and artistic collapse – I am a bankrupt. Do not think that this pitiful cry implies any irony or bitterness towards you. My suffering is so great that I may permit myself to express it since I abstain from accusing anyone of being the author if it but myself.

You have preferred to devote your life and the treasures of your mind and affection to one who is my superior, and, far from blaming you, I approve your action from every point of view and admit you are perfectly right. I swear that the only consoling thought that has from time to time lightened the darkness of my mind and mitigated my external sufferings has been this: at all events Cosima is happy over there . . .

May God protect and bless the mother of the fortunate children to whom she continues to devote herself.

The memories of a true friendship — happy and sad — are there for life.

Barbara Jones, Southsea

Back in the coffee-bar days of the early sixties my schoolfriend Ruth and I were enjoying a 'frothy coffee' when the two young men from the neighbouring table started to talk to us. They were dashingly handsome and elegantly dressed. Their English was very limited and Ruth and I found that our school French came in exceedingly useful — the two young men were from Rome and French was also their second language.

They were students on holiday in Cambridge for two weeks and this was only their second day in England. Ruth and I were about to leave school after doing our 'O' levels, so we were free of studying long enough to meet these two young men several more times before their return to Italy.

As I left school and started work, I saved hard to make a visit to Italy. In 1963, I went on a package tour, alone, at the age of eighteen, to eight European countries in fifteen days. We were to visit Rome for the middle weekend of the fortnight and, on the evening of the party's arrival, Aldo was there at the hotel to meet me. We visited all the sights of Rome together and went out to restaurants and to visit his home.

I was shy about my poor French, but he was kind and gentle – a perfect gentleman all round. I was sad to leave the Eternal City because Aldo had made it magic for me. We continued to write to each other (in French) and photos were exchanged from time to time. News came that he was planning a visit to Cambridge and the day finally arrived when he would spend two weeks with my family. It was a wonderful time and we went to all the colleges – where I also became a tourist in my home town – and to dances and the museum. All too soon the time passed and Aldo left to go home.

We continued to write and exchange photos of the mutual holiday. Our lives followed different paths, but we never lost touch altogether. Five years ago, I went to Rome again and visited a restaurant near his old home and made enquiries about his whereabouts. I was told that he would be along any minute for his regular Sunday lunch there, so I decided to wait for his arrival and surprise him. Boy, was he surprised! We had lunch together and spent my last day in Rome catching up on all the long years since we first met, still in French as before.

Last year, I moved to my first own home, and wrote to tell all my friends of my new address. About two weeks later, a letter came from Rome – from Aldo's mother, whom I had never met in all these years. The letter said, 'I am sorry to have to tell you that Aldo died, very suddenly and unexpectedly, on March 6th.'

He was only fifty-four, and always remained, for me,

a person of magical quality, someone who came from a mysteriously sophisticated city and who was elegant and courteous, gentle and affectionate. Meeting such a person at such a young age as I was then was an impressive event. He has 'been there' in the background of my entire adult life, and now, something wonderful is missing and will always be missing.

Even though the initial romance became a friendship from afar, I certainly miss him in a deep and sad way.

'For stony limits cannot hold love out.'
William Shakespeare, Romeo and Juliet

TO —

Percy Bysshe Shelley (1792–1822)

Music, when soft voices die,
Vibrates in the memory;
Odours, when sweet violets sicken,
Live within the sense they quicken.

Rose leaves, when the rose is dead,
Are heaped for the belovèd's bed;
And so thy thoughts, when thou art gone,
Love itself shall slumber on.

BRIEF ENCOUNTER

Noël Coward (1899–1973)

In a scene full of tension and understatement, two comparative strangers hardly dare admit — even to themselves — what might happen . . .

(*Laura and Alec are having tea in the waiting-room of a suburban railway station.*)

LAURA: Is tea bad for one? Worse than coffee, I mean?

ALEC: If this is a professional interview, my fee is a guinea.

LAURA: Why did you become a doctor?

ALEC: That's a long story. Perhaps because I'm a bit of an idealist.

LAURA: I suppose all doctors ought to have ideals, really — otherwise I should think their work would be unbearable.

ALEC: Surely you're not encouraging me to talk shop?

LAURA: Why shouldn't you talk shop? It's what interests you most, isn't it?

ALEC: Yes, it is. I'm terribly ambitious really, not ambitious for myself so much as for my special pigeon.

LAURA: What is your special pigeon?

ALEC: Preventative medicine.

LAURA: Oh, I see.

ALEC: (*laughing*) I'm afraid you don't.

LAURA: I was trying to be intelligent.

ALEC: Most good doctors, especially when they're young, have private dreams — that's the best part of them; sometimes, though, those get over-professionalised and strangulated and — am I boring you?

LAURA: No — I don't quite understand — but you're not boring me.

ALEC: What I mean is this — all good doctors must be primarily enthusiastic. They must have, like writers and painters and priests, a sense of vocation — a deep-rooted, unsentimental desire to do good.

LAURA: Yes — I see that.

ALEC: Well, obviously one way of preventing disease is worth fifty ways of curing it — that's where my ideal comes in — preventative medicine isn't anything to do with medicine at all, really — it's concerned with conditions, living conditions and common sense and hygiene. For instance, my speciality is pneumoconiosis.

LAURA: Oh dear!

ALEC: Don't be alarmed, it's simpler than it sounds — it's nothing but a slow process of fibrosis of the lung due to the inhalation of particles of dust. In the hospital here there are splendid opportunities for observing cures and making notes, because of the coal-mines.

LAURA: You suddenly look much younger.

ALEC: (*brought up short*) Do I?

LAURA: Almost like a little boy.

ALEC: What made you say that?

LAURA: (*staring at him*) I don't know — yes, I do.

ALEC: (*gently*) Tell me.

LAURA: (*with panic in her voice*) Oh no — I couldn't really. You were saying about the coal-mines.

ALEC: (*looking into her eyes*) Yes — the inhalation of coal-dust — that's one specific form of the disease — it's called anthracosis.

LAURA: (*hypnotised*) What are the others?

ALEC: Chalicosis — that comes from metal-dust — steel-works, you know . . .

LAURA: Yes, of course. Steelworks.

ALEC: And silicosis — stone-dust — that's gold-mines.

LAURA: (*almost in a whisper*) I see. (*There is the sound of a bell.*)

LAURA: That's your train.

ALEC: (*looking down*) Yes.

LAURA: You mustn't miss it.

ALEC: No.

LAURA: (*again with panic in her voice*) What's the matter?

ALEC: (*with an effort*) Nothing — nothing at all.

LAURA: (*socially*) It's been so very nice — I've enjoyed my afternoon enormously.

ALEC: I'm so glad — so have I. I apologise for boring you with those long medical words.

LAURA: I feel dull and stupid, not to be able to understand more.

ALEC: Shall I see you again?

(*There is the sound of a train approaching.*)

LAURA: It's the other platform, isn't it? You'll have to run. Don't worry about me — mine's due in a few minutes.

ALEC: Shall I see you again?

LAURA: Of course — perhaps you could come over to Ketchworth one Sunday. It's rather far, I know, but we should be delighted to see you.

ALEC: (*intensely*) Please — please . . .

(*The train is heard drawing to a standstill . . .*)

LAURA: What is it?

ALEC: Next Thursday — the same time.

LAURA: No — I can't possibly — I . . .

ALEC: Please — I ask you most humbly . . .

LAURA: You'll miss your train!

ALEC: All right. (*He gets up*)

LAURA: Run . . .

ALEC: (*taking her hand*) Good-bye.

LAURA: (*breathlessly*) I'll be there.

ALEC: Thank you, my dear.

A railway carriage, the scent of ripe peaches and the strains of classical music will always bring back special memories to this writer.

SYBIL WHITE, ALNWICK

Towards the end of World War II, I was living with my family in a city in the north of England. I had always been an excellent scholar in French, and when a request for Christmas visits came from the local French aerodrome, my parents willingly extended an invitation.

I was duly allotted our 'French airman', who came with a certificate of good character issued by the camp adjutant. His name was Roger; he was a little older than I, at seventeen, would have wished; but he was well mannered, kindly, and full of wit and humour. Roger and I took long walks with the family dog, and cycle rides into the lovely countryside, and best of all, he took me to concerts of classical music, given by the touring London Philharmonic Orchestra.

I discovered the delights of seeing Eileen Joyce playing Grieg, watching the 'greats' such as Sir Thomas Beecham and Charles Munch conducting; but above all, for me, as a violin student, hearing a young French violinist, Ginette Neveu, playing Beethoven came close to heaven, and her premature death in an air crash robbed the world of a fantastic talent.

Time passed, the horrible war ended, and my lovely Frenchman went home to France, posted to Bordeaux; we wrote regularly, and two years later I managed to take my first holiday abroad to France.

The next few days were passed in an ecstatic haze. Roger met me, and we spent the whole short time together. We walked round that lovely city, fed the fish in the park, went to 'Le Dancing', where I learnt to do the paso doble, drank wine and ate food unknown in 'austerity' Britain, and of course listened to our beloved classical music.

The last day came, we went to the station, and, knowing there really wasn't any future for us, tried to keep the parting light-hearted. Just before the train started off, Roger handed me a bag of peaches and a spray of flowers, and as the train drew away and gathered speed, he stood on the running-board, holding my hand until the very last second, before jumping off at the end of the platform. I can't remember a single moment of the journey back, but even now the scent of ripe peaches brings a pang of memory.

'No, there's nothing half so sweet in life as love's young dream.'
Thomas Moore (1779–1852)

DOCTOR ZHIVAGO

Boris Pasternak (1890–1960)

In the chaos of revolution, Tonya's letter has taken five months to reach her husband, Yury Zhivago. She is unaware that because of the fighting he has been forced to seek refuge in the home of Larissa Fyodorovna – his beloved Lara.

'Yura,' Tonya wrote, 'do you know that we have a daughter? We have christened her Masha in memory of your mother.

'Now about something else. – Several prominent people, professors who belonged to the Cadet party and right-wing socialists, Milyukov, Kizewetter, Kuskova and several others, including your Uncle Kolya, my father and the rest of us, are being deported from Russia.

'This is a misfortune, especially in your absence, but we must accept it and thank God that our exile takes so mild a form at this terrible time when things could have been so much worse for us. If you were here, you would come with us. But where are you? I am sending this letter to Antipova's address; she'll give it to you if she finds you. I am tortured by not knowing if the exit permit we are getting as a family will be extended to you later on, when, if God is willing, you are found. I have not given up believing that you are alive and that you will be found. My heart tells me that this is so, and I trust it. Perhaps by then, by the time you reappear, conditions in Russia will be milder, and you will manage to get a separate visa for yourself, and we shall all be once more together in the same place. But as I write this, I don't myself believe in the possibility of so much happiness.

'The whole trouble is that I love you and that you don't love me. I keep trying to discover the meaning of this judgment on me, to understand it, to see the reason for it. I look into myself, I go over our whole life together and everything I know about myself, and I can't find the beginning, and I can't remember what it is I did and how I brought this misfortune on myself. You have a false, unkindly view of me, you see me in a distorting mirror.

'As for me, I love you. If only you knew how much I love you. I love all that is unusual in you, the inconvenient as well as the convenient, and all the ordinary things which, in you, are made precious to me by being combined in an extraordinary way; your face which is made beautiful by your expression, though perhaps it would be plain without it, your intelligence and your talent which replace your will – for you have no will. All of it is dear to me and I know of no one better than you in the world.

'But listen, this is what I want to say to you. Even if you had been less dear to me, even if I had liked and admired you less, I would still have thought that I loved you, the dreadful fact that I was indifferent would have been hidden from me. Out of sheer terror of inflicting on you such a humiliating, such an annihilating punishment, I would have unconsciously taken care not to realise that I didn't love you. Neither you nor I would ever have known it. My own heart would have hidden it from me, because not to love is almost like murder and I could never have had the strength to deal such a blow to anyone.

'Nothing is definitely settled yet, but we are probably going to Paris. I'll be in those distant lands where you were taken as a child and where Father and my uncle were brought up. Father sends you his greetings. Sasha has grown a lot; he is not particularly good-looking but he is a big, strong boy, and whenever we speak of you he cries bitterly and won't be comforted. I can't go on. I can't stop crying. Well, good-bye. Let me make the sign of the cross over you and bless you for all the years ahead, for the endless parting, the trials, the uncertainties, for all your long, long and dark way. I am not blaming you for anything, I am not reproaching you, make your life as you wish, only so that you are all right.

'Before we left the Urals — what a terrible and fateful place it turned out to be for us — I got to know Larissa

Fyodorovna fairly well. I am thankful to her for being constantly at my side when I was having a difficult time and for helping me through my confinement.

'I must honestly admit that she is a good person, but I don't want to be a hypocrite – she is exactly the opposite of myself. I was born to make life simple and to look for sensible solutions, she – to complicate it and confuse the way.

'God keep you, I must stop. They have come for the letter, and it's time I packed. O Yura, Yura, my dear, my darling, my husband, my children's father, what is happening to us? Do you realise that we'll never, never see each other again? Now I've written it down, do you realise what it means? Do you understand, do you understand? They are hurrying me and it's as if they had come to take me to my death. Yura! Yura!'

Yury finished reading and raised his eyes. They were absent, tearless, dry with grief, emptied by suffering. He neither saw nor was aware of anything round him.

Outside it was snowing. The snow, swept by the wind, fell thicker and thicker, and faster and faster, as if it were trying to catch up with something, and Yury stared out at it, not as if he were looking at the snow, but as if he were still reading Tonya's letter; and as if the whiteness flickering past him were not the small dry snow stars but the blanks between the small black letters, white and endless.

Involuntarily he cried out and clutched his breast. He felt that he was fainting, hobbled the few steps to the sofa and fell down on it unconscious.

GO NOW

Edward Thomas (1878–1917)

Edward Thomas married in 1899 without the knowledge of his parents and his first child was born a year later. He supported his family entirely by his writing until he joined the Army. He was killed on active service in 1917.

Like the touch of rain she was
On a man's flesh and hair and eyes
When the joy of walking thus
Has taken him by surprise:

With the love of the storm he burns,
He sings, he laughs, well I know how,
But forgets when he returns
As I shall not forget her 'Go now'.

Those two words shut a door
Between me and the blessed rain
That was never shut before
And will not open again.

There may well be a time when all good things have to come to an end. But if only she could have stayed on after the chaperone had left!

ALISON PATON, EDINBURGH

When I was seventeen, I lived with a wonderful Spanish family and taught their two daughters English. The summers were perfect and I was asked to a family wedding. Some of the family came from Madrid, and one was a cousin, a Spanish cavalry officer, called Jaime.

The family stayed on for part of the summer and Jaime asked me to go to dinner at a local restaurant. He arrived in the old family Rolls which was chauffeur-driven, and in the back seat was his mother. She was our chaperone for the evening! She never spoke a word, and sat at a separate table. It was a blissful evening: no one holds you and dances like a Spaniard. One feels beautiful and special.

We spent a blissful six weeks together: riding the polo ponies in the hills; stopping at bars for sherry and *tapas*; swimming the horses in the sea; eating out and dancing. After three visits to the same restaurant, I must have passed the test, because our chaperone stayed at home.

I shall never forget that summer and my wonderful Jaime who made me feel so very special.

'If ever thou shalt love, in the sweet pangs of it remember me.'
William Shakespeare, Twelfth Night.

TONIGHT I CAN WRITE

Pablo Neruda (1904–1973)

Pablo Neruda was one of the greatest poets of the twentieth century and winner of the Nobel Prize for Literature.

Tonight I can write the saddest lines.

Write, for example, 'The night is starry
and the stars are blue and shiver in the distance.'

The night wind revolves in the sky and sings.

Tonight I can write the saddest lines.
I loved her, and sometimes she loved me too.

Through nights like this one I held her in my arms.
I kissed her again and again under the endless sky.

She loved me, sometimes I loved her too.
How could one not have loved her great still eyes.

Tonight I can write the saddest lines.
To think that I do not have her. To feel that I have
    lost her.

To hear the immense night, still more immense
    without her.
And the verse falls to the soul like dew to the pasture.

What does it matter that my love could not keep her.
The night is starry and she is not with me.

This is all. In the distance someone is singing. In the
    distance.
My soul is not satisfied that it has lost her.

My sight tries to find her as though to bring her closer
My heart looks for her, and she is not with me.

The same night whitening the same trees.
We, of that time, are no longer the same.

I no longer love her, that's certain, but how I loved
    her.
My voice tried to find the wind to touch her hearing.

Another's. She will be another's. As she was before my
    kisses.
Her voice, her bright body. Her infinite eyes.

I no longer love her, that's certain, but maybe I love
    her.
Love is so short, forgetting is so long.

Because through nights like this one I held her in my
    arms
my soul is not satisfied that it has lost her.

Though this be the last pain that she makes me suffer and
these the last verses that I write for her.

It is for the survivors that war can cause such grief and heartache.

Fleur Walker, Southampton

As a very young person, I had left home to train as a nurse. Very young, keen and hugely patriotic, I worked long hours learning in an operating theatre in a front-line hospital on the south coast. The Queen Alexandra nurses were in France in the field hospitals, giving instant medical treatment to the many casualties of the Normandy landings.

Back in England we prepared dressings and beds were made ready and we knew just what we had to do. On that unforgettable day in June when we heard the waves of planes heading towards France, we all realised that this was what we had trained and prepared for. It was not long before the first casualties reached us. The theatres were busy for twenty-four hours at a stretch. With teams of surgeons from London, we worked non-stop. Limbs were amputated, wounds stitched and burns treated.

Being in such close contact with these brave young men created strong bonds, and the men were very grateful for all that we did for them. Many declared their undying love for their angels, as they called us. I well remember Stevie from Mexico who had volunteered to fight for the Allies. He was badly injured and for a short time I was assigned to look after just him. I became his 'special'. For me, it was a heartbreaking time, as I knew that our task was just to get these men strong enough to travel by train to a safer hospital inland. I realised that these were fragile relationships that fate might break up. Nevertheless, Stevie became very important to me and I blocked out all thoughts of the future.

Then came the news that we were to prepare our patients for their train journey that week. We both felt devastated. Stevie said that nobody else could look after him and I felt that he was my special patient. The surgeons said that Stevie was fit enough to travel and we agreed that I would visit him and that eventually we would be together.

The journey to the station was a nightmare for the two of us and I suspect others. Stevie's rear gunner, who was not so badly injured, promised to keep me informed of Stevie's health and movements. Saying goodbye was awful. Even worse was the ghastly telephone call telling me that Stevie had died. Cruel fate! He, a Mexican, had not even needed to fight to help our beleaguered islands. I shall never forget him. He was my first love and I always remember him when I go near that railway station. I should like to dedicate this letter to the courage of all those brave men like Stevie.

'Absence from whom we love is worse than death,
And frustrate hope severer than despair.'
William Cowper (1731–1800)

WHEN WE TWO PARTED

George Gordon, Lord Byron (1788–1824)

When we two parted
    In silence and tears,
Half broken-hearted,
    To sever for years,
Pale grew thy cheek and cold,
    Colder thy kiss;
Truly that hour foretold
    Sorrow to this.

The dew of the morning
    Sunk chill on my brow—
It felt like the warning
    Of what I feel now.
Thy vows are all broken,
    And light is thy fame;
I hear thy name spoken,
    And share in its shame.

They name thee before me,
   A knell to mine ear;
A shudder comes o'er me—
   Why wert thou so dear?
They know not I knew thee,
   Who knew thee too well:—
Long, long shall I rue thee,
   Too deeply to tell.

In secret we met—
   In silence I grieve,
That thy heart could forget,
   Thy spirit deceive.
If I should meet thee
   After long years,
How should I greet thee?
   With silence and tears.

ROBERT BURNS
(1759–1796) TO AGNES
McLEHOSE

On 30 December 1787, Robert Burns declared that he was ready to hang himself for a young Edinburgh widow. The lady in question was Agnes McLehose, who, despite providing him with the inspiration for many of his best-known lyrics, managed to keep him at arm's length.

MARCH 1793

I suppose, my dear Madam, that by your neglecting to inform me of your arrival in Europe, a circumstance which could not be indifferent to me, as indeed no occurrence relating to you can — you meant to leave me to guess and gather that a correspondence I once had the honour and felicity to enjoy, is to be no more. — Alas, what heavy laden sounds are these – 'no more!' – The wretch who has never tasted pleasure, has never known woe; but what drives the soul to madness, is the recollection of joys that are 'no more!' – But this is not language to the world. – They do not understand it. But, come, ye children of Feeling & Sentiment; ye whose trembling bosom chords ache, to unutterable anguish, as recollection gushed on the heart! Ye who are capable of an attachment, keen as the arrow of Death, and strong as the vigour of Immortal Being – Come! and your ears shall drink a tale – but hush! – I must not, can not tell it! Agony is in the recollection, and frenzy is in the recital!

I present you a book: may I hope you will accept of it. – I dare say you have brought your books with you. – The fourth volume of the Scots Songs is published: I will also send it you.—

Shall I hear from you? But first, hear me! No cold language – no prudential documents – I despise Advice, and scorn Control – If you are not to write such language, such sentiments, as you know I shall wish, shall delight to receive; I conjure you, By wounded Pride! By ruined Peace! By frantic disappointed Passion! By all the many ills that constitute that sum of human woes – A BROKEN HEART! – To me be silent for ever ! ! ! – If you insult me with the unfeeling apothegms of cold-blooded Caution, May all the – but hold – a Fiend could not breath a malevolent wish on the head of MY Angel!

Mind my request! – If you send me a page baptised in

the font of sanctimonious Prudence — By Heaven, Earth and Hell, I will tear it into atoms!—

Adieu! May all good things attend you!

R.B.

SONNET XLII

Edna St Vincent Millay (1892–1950)

One of the best-known American poets of her time, Edna St Vincent Millay was awarded the Pulitzer Prize in 1923.

What lips my lips have kissed, and where, and why,
I have forgotten, and what arms have lain
Under my head till morning; but the rain
Is full of ghosts tonight, that tap and sigh
Upon the glass and listen for reply,
And in my heart there stirs a quiet pain
For unremembered lads that not again
Will turn to me at midnight with a cry.
Thus in the winter stands the lonely tree,
Nor knows what birds have vanished one by one,
Yet knows its boughs more silent than before:
I cannot say what loves have come and gone,
I only know that summer sang in me
A little while, that in me sings no more.

Three decades have not dimmed the memory of a very special evening in Venice.

SUE GARRETT, WHADDON

I had left school and was waiting to go off to university. Colin and I had met earlier in the year and decided to have a holiday together. We both lived in Hampshire at the time, but I was bound for Nottingham and he to continue his architectural studies in Kingston-upon-Thames.

Our arrival in Italy was via the overnight train for Venice. We found a cheap hotel and spent a few hours wandering through the maze of streets and alleyways. It was exactly as I had imagined, with Canaletto views of the canals.

That evening we went in seach of food, ignoring the hotels and restaurants, looking instead for cheap cafés. We had a budget of £1 per day, and the train had already blown a big hole in that. We eventually found a café and dined on a huge plate of spaghetti with a tiny blob of meat sauce. After we had eaten, we strolled around the streets, pausing from time to time to watch the gondolas float by, underneath the bridges. I had recently been introduced to Vivaldi's *Four Seasons* and remember hearing part of 'Summer' coming from an open window at the top of one of Venice's amazing old buildings. Colin was wonderfully romantic and insisted on buying me a small bunch of flowers from one of the shops on the Rialto. I thought my heart would burst! I can remember thinking that whatever happened between Colin and me in the future, that evening would always remain as a very special memory.

Distance, new friends and diverse interests led to us drifting apart the following year, but I have wondered over the past twenty-nine years what happened to that tall, very good-looking, blond, blue-eyed architect, and whether he has the same memory of Venice.

'Being kissed by a man who didn't wax his moustache was — like eating an egg without salt.'
Rudyard Kipling (1865–1936)

REMEMBER

Christina G. Rossetti (1830–1894)

Christina Rossetti was a devout Anglican who rejected two suitors on religious grounds yet began an affair with a married man, the painter and poet William Bell Scott. She never married.

Remember me when I am gone away,
    Gone far away into the silent land;
    When you can no more hold me by the hand,
Nor I half turn to go yet turning stay.
Remember me when no more day by day
    You tell me of our future that you planned:
    Only remember me; you understand
It will be late to counsel then or pray.
Yet if you should forget me for a while
    And afterwards remember, do not grieve:
    For if the darkness and corruption leave
    A vestige of the thoughts that once I had,
Better by far you should forget and smile
    Than that you should remember and be sad.

LADY CHATTERLEY'S LOVER

D.H. Lawrence (1885–1930)

Dear Clifford, I am afraid what you foresaw has happened. I am really in love with another man, and do hope you will divorce me. I am staying at present with Duncan in his flat. I told you he was at Venice with us. I'm awfully unhappy for your sake; but do try to take it quietly. You don't really need me any more, and I can't bear to come back to Wragby. I'm awfully sorry. But do try to forgive me, and divorce me and find someone better. I'm not really the right person for you, I am too impatient and selfish, I suppose. But I can't ever come back to live with you again. And I feel so frightfully sorry about it all, for your sake. But if you don't let yourself get worked up, you'll see you won't mind so frightfully. You didn't really care about me personally. So do forgive me and get rid of me.

Clifford was not *inwardly* surprised to get this letter. Inwardly, he had known for a long time she was leaving him. But he had absolutely refused any outward admission of it. Therefore, outwardly, it came as the most terrible blow and shock to him. He had kept the surface of his confidence in her quite serene.

And that is how we are. By strength of will we cut off our inner intuitive knowledge from admitted consciousness. This causes a state of dread, or apprehension, which makes the blow ten times worse when it does fall.

Clifford was like a hysterical child. He gave Mrs Bolton a terrible shock, sitting up in bed ghastly and blank.

'Why, Sir Clifford, whatever's the matter?'

No answer! She was terrified lest he had had a stroke. She hurried and felt his face, took his pulse.

'Is there a pain? Do try and tell me where it hurts you. Do tell me!'

No answer!

'Oh dear, oh dear! Then I'll telephone to Sheffield for Dr Carrington, and Dr Lecky may as well run round straight away.'

She was moving to the door when he said in a hollow tone: 'No!'

She stopped and gazed at him. His face was yellow, blank, and like the face of an idiot.

'Do you mean you'd rather I didn't fetch the doctor?'

'Yes! I don't want him,' came the sepulchral voice.

'Oh, but Sir Clifford, you're ill, and I daren't take the responsibility. I *must* send for the doctor, or I shall be blamed.'

A pause; then the hollow voice said:

'I'm not ill. My wife isn't coming back.' – It was as if an image spoke.

'Not coming back? You mean her ladyship?' Mrs Bolton moved a little nearer to the bed. 'Oh, don't you believe it. You can trust her ladyship to come back.'

The image in the bed did not change, but it pushed a letter over the counterpane.

'Read it!' said the sepulchral voice.

'Why, if it's a letter from her ladyship, I'm sure her ladyship wouldn't want me to read her letter to you, Sir Clifford. You can tell me what she says, if you wish.'

'Read it!' repeated the voice.

'Why, if I must, I do it to obey you, Sir Clifford,' she said.

And she read the letter.

'Well, I *am* surprised at her ladyship,' she said. 'She promised so faithfully she'd come back!'

The face in the bed seemed to deepen its expression of wild, but motionless distraction. Mrs Bolton looked at it and was worried. She knew what she was up against: male hysteria. She had not nursed soldiers without learning something about that very unpleasant disease.

She was a little impatient of Sir Clifford. Any man in his senses must have *known* his wife was in love with somebody else, and was going to leave him. Even, she was sure, Sir Clifford was inwardly absolutely aware of it, only he wouldn't admit it to himself. If he would have admitted

147

it, and prepared himself for it: or if he would have admitted it, and actively struggled with his wife against it: that would have been acting like a man. But no! he knew it, and all the time tried to kid himself it wasn't so. He felt the devil twisting his tail, and pretended it was the angels smiling on him. This state of falsity had now brought on that crisis of falsity and dislocation, hysteria, which is a form of insanity. 'It comes,' she thought to herself, hating him a little, 'because he always thinks of himself. He's so wrapped up in his own immortal self, that when he does get a shock he's like a mummy tangled in its own bandages. Look at him!'

But hysteria is dangerous: and she was a nurse, it was her duty to pull him out. Any attempt to rouse his manhood and his pride would only make him worse: for his manhood was dead, temporarily if not finally. He would only squirm softer and softer, like a worm, and become more dislocated.

The only thing was to release his self-pity. Like the lady in Tennyson, he must weep or he must die.

A THUNDERSTORM IN TOWN (*A Reminiscence:* 1893)

Thomas Hardy (1840–1928)

She wore a new 'terra-cotta' dress,
And we stayed, because of the pelting storm,
Within the hansom's dry recess,
Though the horse had stopped; yea, motionless
    We sat on, snug and warm.

Then the downpour ceased, to my sharp sad pain
And the glass that had screened our forms before
Flew up, and out she sprang to her door:
I should have kissed her if the rain
    Had lasted a minute more.

Michael Hector, Kidwelly

In 1968, I was stationed in Hong Kong and living in barracks, as my wife had refused to join me there with our son who I hadn't seen since he was a few months old. I was seriously depressed by this state of affairs and took to sitting at a Chinese café, alone. The café was merely a collection of home made tables, orange boxes for stools, bustling with local people selling everything from chickens in wicker baskets to hot sugar cane. The family Chan, who ran the café, had recently been rehabilitated from a fishing sampan life, to the land. Chinese music as full pitch completed the scene.

After some months, a letter was placed in front of me. It had been written by Jose, the middle daughter, a beautiful, lissom girl. She had written the letter with lines from various English songs. She was mystified why I never spoke to her yet played with her little sister Akwai, the four year old. I hadn't thought for a moment that such a stunning looking Chinese girl would have any time for such a lonely Caucasian.

I was touched by her concern, and thus began a friend-ship that eventually turned into love. We were inseparable. Believing that my absent wife had decided to break up the marriage I found love and solace with Jose and her family, proudly escorting this ethereal butterfly in her cheongsam to regimental functions. I was from then on almost treated as one of the family and ate with them at the family table meals one would never find in restaurants.

This second existence abruptly ended when my wife suddenly arrived with my son. Duty was so ingrained and I loved my son so much, so Jose and I tearfully discussed the whole sorry situation with her parents but had to part, but remained very close to each other. Never once did Jose or her family disparage or criticise me. Their courtesy and warmth remained constant.

On our return to the UK I was divorced and so lost both of them. Even now I think a great deal of my Chinese family.

'Hereafter, in a better world than this,
I shall desire more love and knowledge of you.'
William Shakespeare, As You Like It

SONG

William Congreve (1670–1729)

False though she be to me and love,
    I'll ne'er pursue revenge;
For still the charmer I approve
    Though I deplore her change.

In hours of bliss we oft have met:
    They could not always last;
And though the present I regret,
    I'm grateful for the past.

ROMEO AND JULIET
excerpt from Act 3, Scene 2

William Shakespeare (1564–1616)

Romeo and Juliet, those 'star-crossed' lovers in fair Verona, were in fact mere children hardly into their teens, and yet they arrange to be married in secret by Friar Lawrence.

During a street brawl, however, Romeo's friend Mercutio is killed by Juliet's cousin Tybalt. Enraged by this needless death, Romeo kills Tybalt and is banished from Verona.

Blissfully unaware of these events, Juliet waits for night and the return of her lover.

JULIET: Gallop apace, you fiery-footed steeds,
    Towards Phoebus' lodging. Such a waggoner
    As Phaëton would whip you to the west

And bring in cloudy night immediately.
Spread thy close curtain, love-performing night,
That runaways' eyes may wink, and Romeo
Leap to these arms untalked of and unseen.
Lovers can see to do their amorous rites
By their own beauties; or, if love be blind,
It best agrees with night. Come, civil night,
Thou sober-suited matron all in black,
And learn me how to lose a winning match
Played for a pair of stainless maidenhoods.
Hood my unmanned blood, bating in my cheeks,
With thy black mantle till strange love grown bold
Think true love acted simple modesty.
Come night, come Romeo; come, thou day in night,
For thou wilt lie upon the wings of night
Whiter than new snow on a raven's back.
Come, gentle night; come, loving, black-browed night,
Give me my Romeo, and when I shall die
Take him and cut him out in little stars,
And he will make the face of heaven so fine
That all the world will be in love with night
And pay no worship to the garish sun.
O, I have bought the mansion of a love
But not possessed it, and though I am sold,
Not yet enjoyed. So tedious is this day
As is the night before some festival
To an impatient child that hath new robes
And may not wear them.

Enter the Nurse (wringing her hands) with the ladder of cords (in her lap)

                         O, here comes my Nurse,
And she brings news, and every tongue that speaks
But Romeo's name speaks heavenly eloquence.
Now, Nurse, what news? What, hast thou there
The cords that Romeo bid thee fetch?
NURSE *(putting down the cords)* Ay, ay, the cords.
JULIET Ay me, what news? Why dost thou wring thy hands?
NURSE Ah, welladay! He's dead, he's dead, he's dead!
We are undone, lady, we are undone.
Alack the day, he's gone, he's killed, he's dead!
JULIET Can heaven be so envious?
NURSE   Romeo can,
Though heaven cannot. O Romeo, Romeo,
Who ever would have thought it Romeo?
JULIET What devil art thou that dost torment me thus?
This torture should be roared in dismal hell.
Hath Romeo slain himself? Say thou but 'Ay',
And that bare vowel 'I' shall poison more
Than the death-darting eye of cockatrice.
I am not I if there be such an 'Ay',
Or those eyes shut that makes thee answer 'Ay'.
If he be slain, say 'Ay'; or if not, 'No'.
Brief sounds determine of my weal or woe.

ADULTERY SONG

Liz Lochhead (b. 1947)

Chorus
I am nothing
To write home about
I am the best thing in your life
But I am best kept secret
From the kids and the wife

We keep each other's counsel
Find our new confidences sweet,
Ignore each other in crowded rooms
Where even our eyes can't meet.—
Till sick of feeling love sick
We seek temporary cures
Always my place
Never yours.

Chorus
Because I am nothing
To write home about
I am the best thing in your life
But I am best kept secret
From the kids and the wife

We talk of somewhere we'll go sometime
As soon as you can—
Till then I'm snatching stolen time
With a borrowed man.
We salt our suppers with secrecy,
Steal kisses in the park
Then you love me half the night with the light on—
But you keep her in the dark.

Chorus
No I am nothing
To write home about
I am the best thing in your life
But you have to keep me secret
From the kids and the wife

You say you're sorry to leave me
I say it is OK
And skin to skin we cling once more
Then you shower love away,
Take the car keys by my ticking clock
Go and leave me in my bed
With her photo in your wallet—
My phone number in your head.

Chorus
Cause there's nothing
I could phone your home about—
There's the kids and the wife
Even for a matter of life and death
I can't interrupt your life

Chorus
No I am nothing
To write home about
I am the best thing in your life
But I am best kept secret
From the kids and the wife

PART FOUR

Love Everlasting

STOLEN PLEASURE

William Drummond of Hawthornden (1585–1649)

Love everlasting was, for William Drummond, something that continued after the death of his fiancée on the eve of their wedding. Memories of her inspired many of his poems and sonnets.

My sweet did sweetly sleep,
And on her rosy face
Stood tears of pearl, which beauty's self did weep;
I, wond'ring at her grace,
Did all amaz'd remain,
When Love said, 'Fool, can looks thy wishes crown?
Time past comes not again.'
Then did I me bow down,
And kissing her fair breast, lips, cheeks, and eyes,
Prov'd here on earth the joys of paradise.

Despite the double standards of their college authorities, a teacher and her student were eventually able to marry — twice!

CLAIRE GORE, HULL

Our romance began in November 1994, in Changchun, a city in north-eastern China.

I had graduated from Lancaster in July 1994 and, largely to get out of an unwanted relationship, had taken out a student loan to enable me to go and teach English in a Chinese teacher training college.

I was working with an American teacher, so we decided to celebrate Thanksgiving. One of our students, Qiu Dewei, was invited, and by chance we asked when his birthday was. He said that he didn't know — he came from a rural village and was the fifth of seven siblings; his parents were illiterate and couldn't remember any of their birthdays. All he knew was that he was born in the winter, so we decided to celebrate his birthday on Thanksgiving.

The Thanksgiving/birthday party was lovely, and it was perhaps there that everything started. I found myself wanting to talk to Dewei and the feeling was mutual. And yet previously there had been no feeling, not even an inkling of attraction on either side.

We started to meet late at night, outdoors in the pitch black where no one would see us. The temperature was

-20°C to -35°C and yet we would agree a time and meet. Neither of us wanted the college authorities to get wind of our romance. We used to meet near the perimeter wall of campus and spend an hour or two together, and it was the purest, most romantic dating I'd ever had.

It was New Year's Eve before I could finally admit that I had fallen in love. I was ill with flu and Saul (this is Dewei's English name) brought me home from a party I'd been attending in the English Department. In spite of all the risks of being caught, he refused to leave me that night and didn't fall asleep – he spent the night monitoring my fever and worrying. This decision not to return to his dormitory was an enormous risk as he shared a room with eight other students, all of whom would be curious about his whereabouts and, potentially, could 'inform' on him.

His bravery, coupled with the tender concern he showed towards me, left me free of all my anxieties and concerns and from that point, though playing a dangerous game of subterfuge with the college officials, we were together.

We travelled China that first winter vacation and Saul took me to his primitive village where we spent Chinese New Year.

To cut a long story short, Saul and I married this year – twice. We married in England in March at my parents' church in Manchester and I wore a red Chinese dress.

We went back to Changchun four days after our wedding. The college had asked Saul to bring me back since they were really in need of a foreign teacher! However, though the officials knew we were together, they refused to acknowledge it when we arrived.

In the summer after Saul's graduation, we went to his village and celebrated another marriage, complete with sedan, gongs, incense, trumpets and traditional costumes. It was beautiful.

Saul didn't get his diploma. Although the college let him graduate, they refused to send his diploma to him. Obviously they needed me there to teach and so let Saul think they had accepted our relationship. They had, in fact, never accepted it, and were only waiting to punish Saul for falling in love with a foreigner.

Ours has been an intensely romantic, though underground, relationship, and only now are we able to be together without fear.

'Pains of love be sweeter far
Than all other pleasures are.'
John Dryden (1631–1700)

JOHN KEATS (1795–1821) TO FANNY BRAWNE

Keats met Fanny Brawne in 1818. They fell in love and exchanged many letters until his death. Before he died, Keats asked for Fanny's letters to be placed on his grave. After his death, she went into mourning for seven years.

27 July 1819
Sunday Night.

My sweet Girl,

I hope you did not blame me much for not obeying your request of a Letter on Saturday: we have had four in our small room playing at cards night and morning leaving me no undisturb'd opportunity to write. Now Rice and Martin are gone and I am at liberty. Brown to my sorrow confirms the account you give of your own ill health. You cannot conveive how I ache to be with you: how I would die for one hour — for what is in the world? I say you cannot conceive; it is impossible you should look with such eyes upon me as I have upon you: it cannot be. Forgive me if I wander a little this evening, for I have been all day employ'd in a very abstract Poem and I am in deep love with you – two things which must excuse me. I have, believe me, not been an age in letting you take possession of me; the very first week I knew you I wrote myself your vassal; but burnt the Letter as the very first time I saw you I thought you manifested some dislike to me. If you should ever feel for Man at the first sight what I did for you, I am lost. Yet I should not quarrel with you, but hate myself if such a thing were to happen – only I should burst if the thing were not as fine as a Man as you are a Woman. Perhaps I am too vehement, then fancy me on my knees, especially when I mention a part of your Letter which hurt me; you say speaking of Mr Severn 'but you must be satisfied in knowing that I admired you much more than your friend'. My dear love, I cannot believe there ever was or ever could be any thing to admire in me especially as far as sight goes – I cannot be admired, I am not a thing to be admired. You are, I love you; all I can bring you is a swooning admiration of your Beauty. I hold that place among men which snubnos'd brunettes with meeting eyebrows do among women – they are trash to me – unless I should find one among them with a fire in her heart like the one which burns in mine. You absorb me in spite of myself – you alone: for I look not forward with any pleasure to what is call'd being settled in the world; I tremble at domestic cares — yet for you I would meet them, though if it would leave you the happier I would rather die than do so. I have two luxuries to brood over in my walks, your Loveliness and the hour of my death. O that I could have possession of them both in the same minute. I hate the world: it batters too much the wings of my self-will, and would I could take a sweet poison from your lips to send me out of it. From no others would I take it. I am indeed astonish'd to find myself so careless of all charms but yours — remembering as I do the time when even a bit of ribband was a matter of interest with me. What softer words can I find for you after this — what it is I will not read. Nor will I say more here, but in a Postscript answer any thing else you may have mentioned in your Letter in so many words — for I am distracted with a thousand thoughts. I will imagine you Venus to-night and pray, pray, pray to your star like a Heathen.

Your's ever, fair Star,
John Keats

My seal is mark'd like a family table cloth with my Mother's initial F for Fanny: put between my Father's initials. You will soon hear from me again. My respectful Compts to your Mother. Tell Margaret I'll send her a reef of best rocks and tell Sam I will give him my light bay hunter if he will tie the Bishop hand and foot and pack him in a hamper and send him down for me to bathe him for his health with a Necklace of good snubby stones about his Neck.

When a couple are united despite incredible odds, it's hardly surprising they should still be together after nearly thirty years.

LENKA STOKES, CHOBHAM

In 1964, I was a student of English in Czechoslovakia, desperately wanting an English penfriend to practise on. Not knowing quite where to write, I sent a letter simply addressed 'University of London, London, England'. Only one reply came back – from an engineering student named David, then in his first year at University College.

David was interested in politics, so we exchanged letters for two years, but they became less frequent as David became frustrated by my inability to give honest answers in my letters owing to censorship.

In 1966 came the first signs of a gap opening up in the Iron Curtain, so I wasted no time in getting a small vacation job with a firm in Essex. David and I arranged to meet one Sunday afternoon outside Westminster Abbey. We had no idea what the other looked like. David approached many foreign-looking girls only to receive icy stares.

But once we found each other and got talking, we discovered that we both loved visiting art galleries; so off we went to spend an afternoon in the Tate. And in the evening, to my first real Western discothèque.

We continued seeing each other as often as we could,

and soon appreciated that we were in love. As the date of my departure drew near, we realised we could not live without one another, and David proposed to me. At that time, the vision of us being married seemed like a dream which could not possibly come true.

We had no choice but to part and for me to go back to Czechoslovakia. However, we were determined to get married as soon as we finished our studies. We did not know how we would arrange it, since travel into and out of Czechoslovakia was still very strictly controlled.

Easter 1968 was the Prague Spring, when Dubcek brought new freedoms to the Czech people. So David grabbed the opportunity and flew to Czechoslovakia with the intention of asking my father for my hand. To our grief this was refused; my parents felt that Czech girls should not go to live abroad.

Devastated by my parents' reaction, we now had an absolute conviction that we would somehow get together – BUT we had not anticipated that it would take the full might of the Soviet Army! As Russian tanks invaded Czechoslovakia in August 1968, I hastily packed a small case and escaped on the last train to Austria before the borders were closed.

After a month in Vienna, almost penniless, down to seven stone in weight and living with the down-and-outs whilst waiting for a British visa, I arrived in England again, this time for good. David met me at Victoria station, and

I collapsed into his arms with sheer happiness and utter exhaustion.

We got married in January 1969 at a small local registry office. The only attendants were two friends as witnesses. When we told my parents afterwards my father predicted that such a penniless marriage could not possibly survive. The early years were indeed hard financially, but we never ceased to be happy; and so this month we will be celebrating twenty-eight years of a blissfully happy marriage.

'Tho' poor in gear, we're rich in love.'
Robert Burns (1759–1796)

From SUMMER WITH MONIKA

Roger McGough (b. 1937)

ten milk bottles standing in the hall
ten milk bottles up against the wall
next door neighbour thinks we're dead
hasnt heard a sound he said
doesn't know weve been in bed
the ten whole days since we were wed

noone knows and noone sees
we lovers doing as we please
but people stop and point at these
ten milk bottles a-turning into cheese

ten milk bottles standing day and night
ten different thicknesses and
different shades of white
persistent carolsingers without a note to utter
silent carolsingers a-turning into butter

now she's run out of passion
and there's not much left in me
so maybe we'll get up
and make a cup of tea
then people can stop wondering
what theyre waiting for
those ten milk bottles a-queuing at our door
those ten milk bottles a-queuing at our door

A modern day Romeo and Juliet with language problems.

Derek Widenbar, Chesham

It was about ten o'clock on a warm summer evening and I was sitting alone at the café table, feeling utterly dejected. The place was Lido di Jesolo on the Italian Adriatic. More adventurous friends had persuaded me to accompany them there. I was just twenty and it was my first holiday abroad. With great courage, I had that afternoon asked a Swedish girl to join me in the evening, and now I had been stood up!

I had nothing more exciting to do than read a book and have an early night. Suddenly, the silence and my black mood was broken by a clear voice. 'Bonsoir, monsieur.' I looked up into the smiling face of a pretty girl who was staying at the same hotel.

I struggled to find words to persuade her to come with me to one of the local night spots or simply to stroll down the seaside promenade in the moonlight. However, the words never had time to materialise before a lady appeared and spoke in a language that was not French but Italian. Not only was the lady the mother of my new friend but we had been trying to converse in a language that neither of us could speak.

The next day was the penultimate day of my holiday.

On the beach, that morning, Giovanna joined us and I learned that she was from Milan. I could not stay on the beach long because our party had arranged to go on a coach tour to Verona and an opera in the amphitheatre that night. Vanna was urged to come with us and, to my delight, agreed.

Verona is very picturesque and we found it a wonderful place. Vanna and I wandered around enthralled, and soon became lost in each other's company like some modern-day Romeo and Juliet. Just before the performance at the opera, the patrons lit candles, the amphitheatre became a sea of flickering light, and we gazed at it all and at each other enraptured. Something was stirring within us and life for us would never be the same again. The orchestra began playing and the air was filled with the music of Mascagni's *Cavalleria rusticana*. In the darkness, we exchanged our first kiss.

The opera ended to loud applause. Unknown to us, *Cavalleria rusticana* was to be followed by Tchaikovsky's *Swan Lake*. We were panic-stricken. We had promised Vanna's mother that she would be returned safely before midnight. But soon our anxiety gave way to fatigue and we fell asleep on the hard stone seat in each other's arms.

We returned to be confronted by a very angry Italian mother, who whisked her daughter away into the night.

On our last day in Italy, I was very sad because Vanna was nowhere to be seen. After a very lonely day, with only a little while before the coach was due to take us to Venice airport for our overnight flight home, I walked to the sea-facing side of the hotel for one last look at the Adriatic. As I was returning, I heard from on high a voice whispering my name, and looked up to see my beloved on the balcony above. She had been sent to her room on returning and forbidden to see me. However, this modern Juliet had learned the art of climbing down drainpipes and a few minutes later she was in my arms.

There was only time to exchange addresses and for one last, lingering kiss before I had to board the coach. Her tear-stained face smiling up at me as the coach pulled away will never be forgotten.

That Italian holiday romance took place thirty-three years ago but it was only the beginning. For a whole year, I wrote to Vanna in English and she wrote to me in Italian and we each gradually learned to understand what the other was writing. The following year I travelled to Milan and we were reunited. I proposed marriage, was accepted, and her parents gave their blessing. Less than two years later we were married in Milan.

We are still very much in love. My only regrets are that I took Vanna away from her beloved Italy too soon and we do not return very often.

'We are so fond of one another, because our ailments are the same.'
Jonathan Swift (1667–1745)

THE OWL AND
THE PUSSY-CAT

Edward Lear (1812–1888)

Although Edward Lear is best remembered for his nonsense verse, he was such an accomplished painter of animals and landscapes that he gave drawing lessons to Queen Victoria.

The Owl and the Pussy-Cat went to sea
    In a beautiful pea-green boat,
They took some honey, and plenty of money,
    Wrapped up in a five-pound note.
The Owl looked up to the stars above,
    And sang to a small guitar,
'O lovely Pussy! O Pussy, my love,
What a beautiful Pussy you are,
    You are,
    You are!
What a beautiful Pussy you are!'

Pussy said to the Owl, 'You elegant fowl!
    How charmingly sweet you sing!
O let us be married! too long we have tarried:
    But what shall we do for a ring?'
They sailed away for a year and a day,
    To the land where the Bong-tree grows,
And there in a wood a Piggy-wig stood,
With a ring at the end of his nose,
    His nose,
    His nose,
With a ring at the end of his nose.

'Dear Pig, are you willing to sell for one shilling
    Your ring?' Said the Piggy, 'I will.'
So they took it away, and were married next day
    By the Turkey who lives on the hill.
They dined on mince, and slices of quince,
    Which they ate with a runcible spoon;
And hand in hand, on the edge of the sand,
    They danced by the light of the moon,
    The moon,
    The moon,
They danced by the light of the moon.

When the legacy of your love is in the music you love, you have inherited something very special.

ANN RACHLIN, LONDON

It was the first night at sea. In the dining room of the SS *France*, my mother and father made their way to one of the few tables for two. They nodded courteously to a handsome man who sat alone at the next table. The next day, as the liner sailed from New York to Southampton, my parents exchanged greetings with the lone traveller. They discovered he was a symphony conductor from the USA.

In 1937, at the age of 22, he had been chosen and coached by Rachmaninov to bring his Third Piano Concerto to Europe. Now he was travelling to Europe to meet with Rubinstein, Khatchaturian and other famous musicians, with whom he wished to discuss the Van Cliburn International Piano Competition of which he was Chairman of the Jury. My father was thrilled because for years he had been involved with the Leeds International Piano Competition. When their talk turned to children and music, my father proudly took out a newspaper cutting and showed it to the conductor. The large headline read 'Wonder Mum brings music to children'. 'My daughter!' he announced proudly. The conductor stared at the photograph under the headline. 'I conduct a lot of children's concerts in Texas,' he said. 'I would like to meet her.'

When the *France* docked at Southampton, they all three climbed aboard the boat train and travelled together to Waterloo station. I was waiting there to meet my parents. As soon as she saw me, my mother grabbed my hand and said, 'Come with me! We've met an American musician called Ezra who wants to meet you.'

Weaving her way through the piles of luggage, she led me towards this handsome man with laughing eyes. We shook hands. The next day, my parents invited me to lunch. I walked into the restaurant and there was Ezra with my parents. My father kissed me and so did my mother. Behaving totally out of character, I turned to Ezra and said, 'Aren't you going to kiss me?'

That was it. In that moment we fell in love and we were married one year after that first meeting on Waterloo station.

We travelled the world together. For both of us it was a second marriage and we enjoyed twenty-five happy years. Together we brought the love of classical music into the lives of thousands of children through our concerts in the USA, Australia and England.

Ezra was eighteen years older than me but there seemed to be no age difference between us. We shared a great love of children and music. Then three years ago, when our doctor told us that Ezra had to have major surgery, seeing my forlorn face, Ezra said, 'Don't be sad. I will never leave you. Music is where I live and you will always find me there in the music I have left for you. Just switch me on and I'll be there!'

He never came out of hospital. He died but he has not really gone. I have only to turn on my CD player and hear him playing the piano or conducting an orchestra and I know he is there and I am never alone. It is exactly thirty years since we met at the station. Ezra used to laugh and boast how he met his mother-in-law before he met his wife.

'No sooner met, but they looked; no sooner looked but they loved; no sooner loved but they sighed; no sooner sighed but they asked one another the reason; no sooner knew the reason but they sought the remedy.'
William Shakespeare, As You Like It

SONNET No. LVIII

Michelangelo Buonarroti (1475–1564)

Sculptor, painter, architect and creator of the frescoes in the Sistine Chapel, Michelangelo also wrote many beautiful sonnets, seven of which have been set to music by Benjamin Britten.

When to my inward eyes, both weak and strong,
The idol of my heart appears, I know
That always in between us death will go:
It frightens me as it drives me along.

Yet, strangely, such an outrage gives me hope
And I take courage from so rare a fate.
Indomitable love moves in great state
And thus he puts his strong defences up:

Dying, he says, can never happen twice,
Nor is one born again. If a man dies
By fire when he already is aflame

With burning love, then death can do no harm.
Such love's the magnet of all burning hearts
Which, purged, returns to God from where it starts.

VITA SACKVILLE-WEST (1892–1962) TO VIRGINIA WOOLF (1882–1941)

Vita Sackville-West wrote a series of love letters to Virginia Woolf during her travels as a diplomat's wife.

Milan (posted in Trieste)
Thursday 21 January 1927

. . . I am reduced to a thing that wants Virginia. I composed a beautiful letter to you in the sleepless nightmare hours of the night, and it has all gone: I just miss you, in a quite simple desperate human way. You, with all your undumb letters, would never write so elementary a phrase as that; perhaps you wouldn't even feel it. And yet I believe you'll be sensible of a little gap. But you'd clothe it in so exquisite a phrase that it would lose a little of its reality. Whereas with me it is quite stark: I miss you even more than I could have believed; and I was prepared to miss you a good deal. So this letter is just really a squeal of pain. It is incredible how essential to me you have become. I suppose you are accustomed to people saying these things. Damn you, spoilt creature; I shan't make you love me any the more by giving myself away like this – But oh my dear, I can't be clever and stand-offish with you: I love you too much for that. Too truly. You have no idea how stand-offish I can be with people I don't love. I have brought it to a fine art. But you have broken down my defences. And I don't really resent it.

SONNET No. 75

William Shakespeare (1564–1616)

So are you to my thoughts as food to life,
Or as sweet-seasoned showers are to the ground;
And for the peace of you I hold such strife
As 'twixt a miser and his wealth is found:
Now proud as an enjoyer, and anon
Doubting the filching age will steal his treasure;
Now counting best to be with you alone,
Then bettered that the world may see my pleasure;
Sometime all full with feasting on your sight,
And by and by clean starvèd for a look;
Possessing or pursuing no delight
Save what is had or must from you be took.
　　Thus do I pine and surfeit day by day,
　　Or gluttoning on all, or all away.

Who would have thought a blood test would ever lead to a happy and successful marriage?

Nicky Goldberg, Liverpool

In 1985 I was a newly qualified midwife, working in a Liverpool hospital, whilst preparing to become a nun; in fact I was due to enter the convent in October. One morning, the phone rang and a male voice asked me to check some blood results. I was unable to decipher the writing, and suggested that this person come and check for himself.

I continued with my work, and was giving out medicines when I saw him disappearing off the ward. I smiled at him and that was that.

At lunch-time, I was 'handing over' to the afternoon staff when the phone rang. It was the same voice enquiring if I was the staff nurse he had seen on the early shift. On hearing 'yes', he asked if I would think him terribly forward if he asked me out to dinner. I was acutely embarrassed, made more so by the fact that the afternoon staff were watching my blushes, and were all ears.

To end the conversation I agreed to meet him, in as public a place as possible. We met, had a lovely time, and I knew then that this man was going to change my life.

After only two weeks we both knew that this was

serious, and that we wanted to spend our lives together. We overcame some difficulties – our religions were so different (me Catholic, he Jewish) – but we were married some nine months later (with the blessings of my former convent).

Two years later, our first son, Graham Robert, was born, and a year after that Peter Richard. We will have been married now for twelve years, and our love grows stronger each year.

To think that had it not been for an indecipherable blood form we would not have met!

'We love being in love, that's the truth on't.'
William Makepeace Thackeray (1811–1863)

WHEN YOU ARE OLD

W.B. Yeats (1865–1939)

When you are old and grey and full of sleep,
And nodding by the fire, take down this book,
And slowly read, and dream of the soft look
Your eyes had once, and of their shadows deep;

How many loved your moments of glad grace,
And loved your beauty with love false or true,
But one man loved the pilgrim soul in you,
And loved the sorrows of your changing face;

And bending down beside the glowing bars,
Murmur, a little sadly, how Love fled
And paced upon the mountains overhead
And hid his face amid a crowd of stars.

Unruly hair and a cheeky face are not the usual ingredients for a fairytale romance . . .

JULIA WATNEY, OXFORD

Listening to the choirboys at Christmas always reminds me of a particular choirboy I once heard a long time ago, and whom I'm unlikely to forget.

The story starts when I was ten. It was the nineti-eth birthday of Sir Winston Churchill and there was a celebration which was broadcast on TV. The choir of Churchill's old school sang a greeting which included a solo verse specially written for the occasion. I noticed the solo choirboy, because he seemed so different from the usual droopy choirboys: rather spirited, a bit cheeky in fact, with untidy hair. I took so much interest in him that my family started to tease me. Of course I never expected to meet him.

Ten years passed. I was now at Reading University, playing the violin in the orchestra for a concert. I recall being rather annoyed because late-comers were stealing in during the performance and sitting in the front row of the Great Hall, just in front of us. One of them was so close he nearly knocked over my music stand! However, during the party that followed he sought me out and told me that he had been glad he had arrived late, otherwise he would never have got such a good view of me in particular! I was a bit mollified, and we danced together, though when he told me that he was hoping to find a floor to spend the night on because he was far too drunk to drive back home that evening, I thought that was the oldest trick in the book, and that he was decidedly cheeky!

As we gradually got to know each other better, I discovered that he was none other than the same cheeky choirboy I had seen on TV. His voice had broken, of course, some time ago, but his hair was still a mess! We thought what a coincidence it was that each of us had first noticed and admired the other while performing music. We have now been married for many years and have two musical, and cheeky, children.

'A love match was the only thing for happiness, where the parties could any way afford it.'
Maria Edgeworth (1767–1849)

WOLFGANG AMADEUS MOZART (1756–1791) TO CONSTANZE

In 1782, Mozart married a cheerful but relatively nondescript young woman, who would bear him six children and outlive him by over fifty years. His letters to her — after nine years of marriage — were both endearing and passionate.

Vienna
6 June. 1791

I have this moment received your dear letter and am delighted to hear that you are well and in good spirits. Madame Leutgeb has laundered my nightcap and neck-tie, but I should like you to see them! Good God! I kept on telling her, *'Do let me show you how she (my wife) does them!'* — But it was no use. I am delighted that you have a good appetite — but whoever gorges a lot, must also shit a lot — no, walk a lot, I mean. But I should not like you to take *long walks* without me. I entreat you to follow my advice exactly, for it comes from my heart. Adieu — my love — my only one. Do catch them in the air — those 2999½ little kisses from me which are flying about, waiting for someone to snap them up. Listen, I want to whisper something in your ear – and you in mine – and now we open and close our mouths – again – again and again – at last we say: 'It is all about Plumpi – Strumpi—' Well, you can think what you like – that is just why it's so convenient. Adieu. A thousand tender kisses. Ever your

Mozart

As everyone knows, the way to a woman's heart is to throw flowers to her leading man . . .

Philip Christey, London

My job involved arranging visits for American tourists to London. I was in need of outgoing, friendly people to meet the clients at airports, arrange sightseeing tours and theatre visits. A friend of mine told me she knew an out-of-work actress who was looking for work and thought she would fit the bill perfectly.

As soon as Jessica walked into my office with a warm handshake and a wide friendly smile I felt she would be perfect for the job. I was soon totally smitten, and eventually I plucked up courage to ask her out. I was gently but firmly rebutted. To add to my agony, Jessica was offered an acting job and within days she had walked out of my life.

Seven long years passed until one day I read a theatre review of a play that had just opened at the Theatre Royal, Windsor. The play was *Four Hearts, Doubled* by William Douglas-Home, and highly praised in the review was Jessica for her performance as an accomplished bridge player.

Consumed with curiosity, I booked a ticket. I sat spellbound for two hours as Jessica's spectacular talent captivated the audience. The clock had suddenly been turned back and I drove home in a daze.

I realised that I would not get Jessica out of my mind, and I had to make another attempt to see her again. There was only one thing for it. The next morning I telephoned the theatre and booked a box overlooking the stage. At the end of yet another tremendous performance I threw a red rose out of the box, only to see it fall on to the lap of a lady in the front row of the audience! Jessica and the cast hadn't even noticed.

I knew I had to persevere. I went back two nights later and again hurled the rose. To my dismay it hit the leading man, and this time the whole cast looked up to the box to see me sitting there alone! I wanted to crawl under my chair with embarrassment.

I promised myself that I would never set foot in the theatre again, and I was hurrying out of the box and out of the foyer when I heard my name called. It was Jessica! She was laughing and asked would I like to come backstage for a glass of wine?

This time, to my utter delight, the attraction became mutual.

Jessica has given up theatre to raise our three beautiful

young children, and if any of them decide to become an actor they have my full support!

'Therefore love moderately; long love doth so;
Too swift arrives as tardy as too slow.'
William Shakespeare, Romeo and Juliet

GIVING UP SMOKING

Wendy Cope (b. 1945)

There's not a Shakespeare sonnet
Or a Beethoven quartet
That's easier to like than you
Or harder to forget.

You think that sounds extravagant?
I haven't finished yet—
I like you more than I would like
To have a cigarette.

EPILOGUE

Robert Harvey was one of many listeners who heard Kate Harwood's letter (Prologue) read out on the Classic Romance *programme of 17 October 1992 . . .*

ROBERT HARVEY, CHESHIRE

Two years ago, shortly after your programme went on air, you read out a moving letter from Kate Harwood from Leeds. I wrote to Classic FM and you passed my enquiry on to Kate.

So started six months of regular correspondence during which our friendship grew as we found out more about each other's backgrounds, interests, thoughts and hopes for the future.

Our first meeting took place in February of last year with a visit to Buxton Opera House for a magnificent performance of *La Bohème* by the touring Milan Opera Company. Kate must have wondered what sort of idiot she was associating with since I cried nearly all the way through!

Afterwards I drove her back to Leeds, prepared a meal

while she organised herself for school the next day, and we sat up until all hours getting to know each other better. We had made no definite arrangements for a second meeting but within days we were writing to each other suggesting that we get together as soon as possible.

Since then our early friendship has developed through mutual trust and admiration into a very sincere, caring and truly loving relationship. We share so many common interests of which love of classical music, opera and choral music forms a major part. Just as important, perhaps, we encourage each other's personal interests and hobbies and support each other at every opportunity.

Most of all we work at, and protect, our relationship, as it's the most precious thing we have. We operate as a real partnership – differences and disagreements are sorted out by discussion with the emphasis on respecting and considering each other. As a result, we have enjoyed a fantastic eighteen months or so of wonderful teamwork, done many new things together, experienced some lovely trips and journeys, had super holidays and just love being together.

Kate is the most kind and caring person anyone could imagine; she has a great sense of humour and will have a go at anything and is lovely to be with. So much so that I hate being away from her. I know she feels the same.

There is however a solution to this dilemma. Although marriage has never been discussed as such, it is my intention to propose to Kate shortly – and what better time than the second anniversary of our first contact through the *Classic Romance* programme. This corresponds to Sunday, 16 October. So wish me luck!

Whatever the outcome, and regardless of what the future holds for us, we are grateful for the happy times we have enjoyed together since we met through the channel provided by your Sunday morning broadcast.

On 16 October 1994 Robert took Kate to the Classic FM studios for a seemingly casual visit. During the live broadcast of the Classic Romance *programme, he proposed marriage and, in front of nearly a million witnesses, was accepted. The music request was for the love duet from* La Bohème. *Robert was not the only one in the studio in tears.*

It was this programme which won the silver at the 1995 Sony Awards.

Classic Romance Top Twenty Most Popular Requests

1. Rachmaninov: *Piano Concerto No.2*
2. Mascagni: *Intermezzo* from *Cavalleria Rusticana*
3. Debussy: *Clair de lune*
4. Mozart: *Clarinet Concerto in A*
5. Vaughan Williams: *The Lark Ascending*
6. Bizet: 'Au Fond du Temple Saint' from *The Pearl Fishers*
7. Rimsky Korsakov: *Scheherazade*
8. Widor: Toccata in F (From Organ Symphony No.5)
9. Rodrigo: *Concerto de Aranjuez*
10. Tchaikovsky: *Romeo and Juliet* Fantasy Overture
11. Mozart: Overture to *The Marriage of Figaro*
12. Mendelssohn: The *Hebrides Overture*
13. Puccini: 'O Soave Fanciulla' from *La Boheme*
14. Beethoven: *'Moonlight' Sonata*
15. Barber: *Adagio for Strings*
16. James Horner: Soundtrack to *Titanic*
17. Khachaturian: *Adagio of Spartacus and Phrygia* from *Spartacus*
18. Beethoven: *Symphony Number 6* 'Pastoral'
19. Verdi: Overture to *The Force of Destiny*
20. Saint-Saens: *Symphony No 3*

Acknowledgements

I would like to thank Rupert Lancaster of Hodder & Stoughton for having faith in the book from the start, and for the shared interest in social history; Charlotte Barton, also from Hodder, for her impeccable telephone manner; Robert O'Dowd and Kate Sampson from Classic FM for their invaluable support. And to my wife Anne and our three children, Sally, Lucy and Edward, for letting me work on Sunday morning for the last six years without complaint.

— *Nick Bailey*

Papermac for *Thunderstorm In Town* from *The Complete Poems* by Thomas Hardy.

Laurence Pollinger Limited and the Estate of Frieda Lawrence Ravagli for the extract from *Lady Chatterley's Lover* by D. H. Lawrence.

Polygon for *Adultery Song* by Liz Lochhead.

Tonight I Can Write by Pablo Neruda, translated by W. S. Merwin from *Pablo Neruda Selected Poems* edited by Nathaniel Tarn, published by Jonathan Cape.

A. P. Watt on behalf of Michael Yeats for *When You Are Old* from *The Collected Poems* of W. B. Yeats.

Summer With Monika, reprinted by permission of The Peters Fraser And Dunlop Group Limited on behalf of: Roger McGough; Copyright as printed in the original volume.

The Letters Of Vita Sackville-West to Virgina Woolf edited by Louise de Salvo and Mitchell A. Leaska, published by Hutchinson.

Jamaica Inn: Reproduced with permission of Curtis Brown Ltd, London, on behalf of The Chichester Partnership. Copyright Daphne du Maurier.

Letter from Leoš Janáček to Kamila Stosslova from *Intimate Letter*. Translated by Patrick and Jaroslava Lambert Marginalia Press (Ippon Books).

Faber and Faber Ltd for *The Confirmation* by Edwin Muir from *Collected Poems*.

Faber and Faber Ltd for *Valentine* from *Serious Concerns* by Wendy Cope.

Faber and Faber Ltd for *Giving Up Smoking* from *Making Cocoa For Kingsley Amis* by Wendy Cope.

Faber and Faber Ltd for *Alban Berg: Letters to his Wife*, translated by Bernard Grun.

Brief Encounter. Copyright Carlton Film Distributors Ltd. Licensed by Carlton International Media Ltd.

To be published in November 1998

THE CLASSIC FM BOOK OF MUSICAL ANECDOTES, NOTES AND QUOTES

Henry Kelly and John Foley
Foreword by Lesley Garrett

'Musical people are so absurdly unreasonable. They always want one to be perfectly dumb at the very moment when one is longing to be absolutely deaf.' *Oscar Wilde*

'I spend up to six hours a day waving my arms about, and if everyone else did the same they would stay much healthier.' *Sir Malcolm Sargent*

'People are wrong when they say that opera is not what it used to be. It *is* what it used to be. That is what is wrong with it.' *Noel Coward*

Henry Kelly and John Foley have compiled a rich symphony of anecdotes, notes and quotes from the world of classical music – composers, conductors, soloists, instruments, and their critics – from batons to Beethoven, maracas to *Meistersinger*, Verdi to violas, with an entertaining preface by celebrated singer Lesley Garrett.

Already Available

CLASSIC FM
ONE HUNDRED FAVOURITE POEMS

Introduction and biographies of the poets by Mike Read.

Here are the works chosen by Classic FM listeners in the poll to discover their favourite poems. This is a rich and varied collection: here are not only the famous poems you would expect to find – and all the famous poets – but also some wonderful less well-known works, together with biographies of all the poets by Mike Read.

Includes work by Betjeman, Kipling, Shakespeare, Tennyson, Yeats, Wordsworth, Hardy, Larkin, Brooke, Keats, Auden, Rossetti, Browning, Hopkins, Housman, Burns, Donne, Milton, Masefield, Frost and many others.

An audio tape and CD to accompany this book are produced by Hodder Headline Audiobooks.